Conflict in the
Persian Gulf

Conflict in the Persian Gulf

Edited by Murray Gordon

Facts On File
460 Park Avenue South, New York, N.Y. 10016

Conflict in the Persian Gulf

Library of Congress Cataloging in Publication Data

Main entry under title:

Conflict in the Persian Gulf.

  (Checkmark books)
  Includes index.
  1. Persian Gulf region—Politics and government.
I. Gordon, Murray.
DS326.C67   327'.0953'6   80-13216
ISBN 0-87196-158-X

9 8 7 6 5 4 3 2 1
PRINTED IN
THE UNITED STATES OF AMERICA

Contents

Introduction

The Persian Gulf is a region of immense importance to the United States and its Western allies. The bountiful oil resources of Saudi Arabia, Iran and Iraq are essential to the West and will remain indispensable until economically viable alternative sources of energy become available. This is not likely to begin happening until the end of the century. With the exception of England and Norway, which now draw most of their oil from the North Sea, the rest of Western Europe and, to an increasing extent, the United States, are dependent on Persian Gulf and Middle East oil; Japan, which ranks after the United States as the second most powerful industrial nation in the West, but which has virtually no energy sources of its own, imports approximately ninety *per cent* of its oil from the Persian Gulf. In the event the Gulf were lost to the West, or its oil would cease to be available, there is no other country or group of countries that could make up the shortfall. The hard reality is that without continuous assured access to the oil fields of the Gulf, the factories of the Western democracies would soon grind to a halt, causing economic upheaval that would endanger the very fabric of Western society.

The Gulf's importance has also been reflected in the key role assigned to it by Western strategists in protecting Western interests in the Middle East and South Asia. It was largely for this reason that the United States helped organize, in the mid-1950s, the Central Treaty Organization (initially known as the Baghdad Pact). The mission of the Baghdad Pact was to deter the Soviet Union from making a military move against the Middle East or gaining access to warm-water ports in the Indian Ocean, a Russian goal going back to czarist times. Although some of the reasons behind the creation of this defense alliance have lost their validity, others have retained great significance for the United States. Washington would be deeply concerned if the Soviets succeeded in gaining access to warm-water ports in the region, particularly in the light of recent developments in Iran and Afghanistan. Central to American foreign policy today is the establishment of new military arrangements that would insulate the Gulf from East-West rivalries and promote political stability in the region.

In the past, the shah of Iran, Mohammed Riza Pahlevi, had played a central role in the realization of these aims. His country was the linchpin of the Central Treaty Organization, which also included Turkey and Pakistan. With the quantum leap in oil prices in 1973, the shah embarked on a vast military buildup program and, with American encouragement, became the self-proclaimed gendarme of the Persian Gulf. He had extracted from Iraq in 1975 an agreement for the equal division of the Shatt al Arab estuary, which provided access to the Persian Gulf. The Shatt al Arab heretofore had been under Baghdad's complete control. The shah thereafter used his growing military power to extend his influence throughout the Gulf. At the request of the sultan of Oman, he dispatched military forces into this strategically located country to put down a Marxist-inspired rebellion in Dhofar province. And in staking out this position of leadership, the shah developed a tacit alliance with Saudi Arabia, which despite some misgivings about the shah's imperial pretensions and support of Israel, strongly endorsed the objective of promoting stability in the region. With their vast oil wealth and weak armed forces, the Saudis had every reason to suspect that hostile forces inside the region and without had designs on their country. The Saudis watched anxiously as the Soviets gained a toehold in Marxist Southern Yemen (the People's Democratic Republic of Yemen), a client state of Moscow's which, from time to time, became embroiled in conflict with neighboring Yemen Arab Republic (sometimes called Northern Yemen) with a view to unifying the two countries under communist rule.

The shah's role of policeman of the Persian Gulf fitted in well with American strategic interests in the region. By the time he had undertaken this security duty, the British had given up their century-old task of protector of the Gulf by withdrawing the last of their military forces from east of Suez. Unless suitable defensive measures were adopted, it was feared, the military vacuum might be filled by the Soviets or by Iraq, which was linked to the Kremlin by treaty ties. The United States, then ending its involvement in the Vietnam war, was in no position to adopt a military position for the defense of the region. Public opinion, traumatized by the long and costly Vietnamese conflict, would be strongly opposed to such a step. Not unmindful of these political constraints, President Richard Nixon and his chief foreign policy adviser, Henry Kissinger, evolved a new policy that would provide a degree of protection to the Gulf without directly involving the United States. Under this approach, which became known as the "Nixon Doctrine," the United States agreed to have the shah take over primary responsibility for the defense of the Gulf. As part of the arrangement, President Nixon agreed to sell to Iran almost any weapons system in the American arsenal short of nuclear arms.

Whatever its shortcomings, and these were substantial, the arrangement was not without benefits to Iran. A considerable measure of stability was achieved for the region as a whole. A militarily strong Iran had little to fear from any neighbors that might be tempted to win over its oil wealth. The country pursued a vigorous modernization program based on the familiar western models; development, as a result, tended to be concentrated in the large urban areas and paid little heed to the country's agricultural needs. As a result, relatively small numbers of people benefited from the country's oil wealth. Exacerbating this situation was the failure of the shah to allow for the development of political institutions that could allow the country to achieve a degree of democracy and citizen participation in decision-making processes. The pervasive corruption, which reached into the royal family, and the dreaded secret police further served to alienate the people, even those who had derived considerable benefits from the system. As it turned out, the security the shah had hoped to gain for his throne and country through an active foreign policy failed to materialize because he lacked the necessary popular support at home.

As for the United States, the arrangement with the shah yielded substantial gains in the military, economic and energy spheres. Political stability in the Gulf was achieved at little cost to the United States. The United States became the primary supplier of military goods to Iran—weapons that became the new symbol of an American presence in the region. Along with these weapons went a small army of military and technical advisers whose role served to reenforce Washington's primary position in the country. And in order to pay for the sophisticated weapons systems that he so insistently sought from the United States, the shah sold five million barrels of oil a day to the West. This provided him with the money he required to underwrite his ambitious military and development programs and, at the same time, insured that ample supplies of oil would be available to the West.

With the overthrow of the shah in early 1979, American policy in the region collapsed. No sooner had the Ayatollah Ruhollah Khomeini come to power in Iran than he announced that his country would no longer serve as the watchman of the Gulf and that it would no longer be associated with CENTO (the Central Treaty Organization). Iran, he went on, would cut back sharply its arms purchases from the United States and with this, the amount of oil it would sell to the West. Henceforth, the Iranian religious leader said, his country would stand clear of the two power blocs, ending its long and close association with the United States. With the departure of the shah, the basis of American political influence in Iran ceased to exist. This development pointed up a major flaw in American policy in the Gulf: it was tied to the fate of single individual who, as it turned out, had compromised his own position in the country. When the shah went, the policies that were identified with him, domestic and foreign, also went out of the window.

Since the shah's overthrow, the Persian Gulf has been wracked by continuous violence and instability: ethnic insurgency and political instability in Iran, warfare between the two Yemens, the seizure of the Grand Mosque in Mecca by opponents of the Saudi government and, finally, the Iraqi invasion of Iran. In one way or another, many of these developments are tied to the mounting religious fervor that has been sweeping the lands of Islam in the wake of the Iranian revolution. The Ayatollah Khomeini's dramatic appearance on the world scene did not begin the trend, nor has it developed a cohesive force. Its intensity, its goals and its tactics vary as widely as the geography and history of the world's 700 million to 800 million Muslims. But the movement is tangible and growing. It rouses fear in both the regimes that thought themselves solidly anchored in orthodox tradition and in those that believed themselves immunized through social revolution.

Much of the instability in the Gulf may be traced to the nature of the Islamic religion practiced in Iran. The deep social anger in Iran at the shah, at the United States and even against certain of the adjoining Arab countries has assumed an air of fanaticism in Islam's Shi'ite expression. Shi'ites,

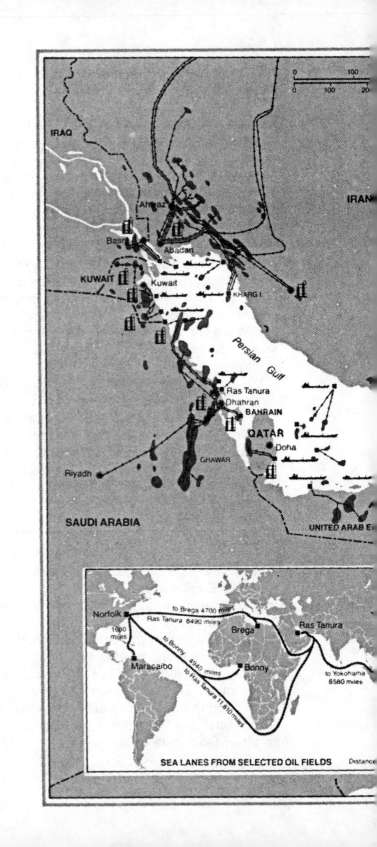

Persian Gulf

IRAQ

Ahwaz

Basra

Abadan

IRAN

KUWAIT

Kuwait

KHARG I.

Ras Tanura

Dhahran

BAHRAIN

QATAR

Doha

Riyadh

GHAWAR

SAUDI ARABIA

UNITED ARAB E

Norfolk

to Brega 4700 miles
Ras Tanura 8490 miles

Brega

Ras Tanura

1680
miles

to Bonny 4940 miles

Maracaibo

to Ras Tanura 11,810 miles

Bonny

to Yokohama
8580 miles

SEA LANES FROM SELECTED OIL FIELDS

Distance

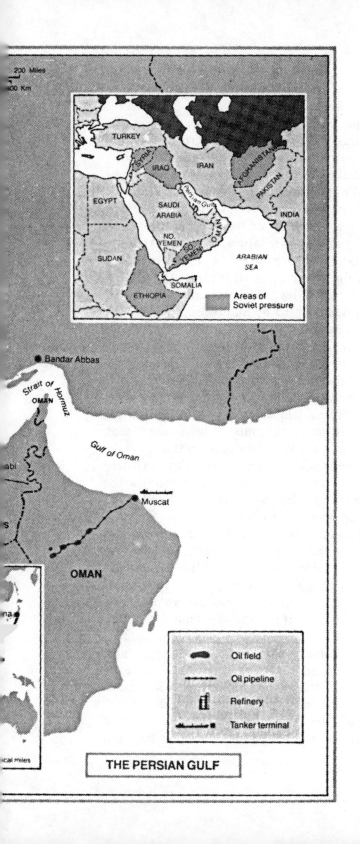

200 Miles
00 Km

TURKEY

SYRIA
IRAQ
IRAN
AFGHANISTAN
PAKISTAN

EGYPT
SAUDI
ARABIA
OMAN
INDIA

Persian Gulf

NO.
YEMEN
SO.
YEMEN

SUDAN

ARABIAN
SEA

SOMALIA

ETHIOPIA

Areas of
Soviet pressure

● Bandar Abbas

Strait of Hormuz
OMAN

Gulf of Oman

Muscat

OMAN

na

abi

s

Oil field

Oil pipeline

Refinery

Tanker terminal

cal miles

THE PERSIAN GULF

who make up ten per cent of Islam, tend toward a passion-
ate, activist religious life and flirtation with martyrdom
(they have been known to commit suicide accidentally by
bashing and mutilating themselves in mourning for their
founder, Husain, the slaughtered grandson of the prophet).
Shi'ites also prefer charismatic leaders; in Iran they seem to
be forever parading the portrait of their Imam Khomeini.
The special ferocity and condensation of the will that are
evident in the Iranian revolution owe much to this tendency
toward the cult of the personality. In contrast to Iran, the
only country where the Shi'ites hold power, most of the rest
of the Muslim world is peopled by Sunnis, followers of the
original tradition, or Sunna. The distinction between Sunnis
and Shi'ites is, according to some scholars of Islam, much
greater than that between, say, Roman Catholics and Pro-
testants. It is one of the most basic of many differences that
make it not only inadvisable but impossible to generalize
about Islam as if it were a single coherent bloc. Just as the
communist world includes antagonists (the Soviet Union
and China), the Islamic world is very much fragmented. In
1979, Northern Yemen (Sana) and Southern Yemen (Aden)
fought a war; Morocco and Algeria have been fighting in the
western Sahara; and in 1980 Iraq and Iran became embroiled
in a no-holds-barred war in the Gulf.

The historic cleavage between the dominant Sunni and
minority Shi'ite sects has worked to enhance the political
power of the Shi'ite religious authorities in Iran. On seizing
power, this religious group has not been loath to use this
power. It incorporated into the new constitution a provision
making Iran a Muslim state of the Shi'ite persuasion despite
the fact that many of the politically restive minorities that
have been seeking autonomy, notably the Kurds and Arabs,
are Sunnis. This insensitivity has served to alienate even
further these and other ethnic minorities from the Khomeini
revolution. The revolutionary government in Teheran has
encouraged fellow Shi'ites in neighboring Iraq, Bahrain and
Kuwait to support the goals of Khomeini. This has sent

shock waves through Iraq and the conservative Arab
monarchies and shiekhdoms in the Gulf. Arab governments,
with few exceptions, have been fearful that Khomeini is bent
on exporting his revolution, which could pose a serious
challenge to their own rule. The heads of the Arab Gulf
states are, without exception, Sunnis. In Iraq, President
Saddam Hussein, a Sunni, rules over a state in which the
majority of the population is Shi'ite. Similarly, a majority of
the people in Bahrain are also of the Shi'a profession,
although the leadership is Sunni. And in the eastern part of
Saudi Arabia, there is a small but increasingly vocal Shi'ite
population, many of whose adherents work in the nearby oil
fields. By and large, the Shi'ites are said to believe that they
have little meaningful voice in the political process and have
a disproportionately smaller share of the benefits of development. Should this population pay heed to the revolutionary appeals coming from Teheran, the result could produce
profound consequences for the political stability of the
entire region. Iraq's decision to go to war against Iran in
September 1980 was, in part, inspired by a desire to discredit
Khomeini and weaken his appeal to the country's Shi'ite
populace.

The Soviet invasion of Afghanistan and the Persian Gulf
war involving Iraq and Iran have enormously complicated
the task confronting the United States of promoting peace
and stability in the region. While these goals were clear
enough, the means of realizing them were far from certain. It
remained to be seen whether President Jimmy Carter's
tough stance against the Soviet move into Afghanistan—
and whatever steps his successor, Ronald Reagan, would
take—would deter the U.S.S.R. from taking any threatening political or military initiatives in the Persian Gulf. It was
far from certain whether the Soviet Union, which could
rapidly deploy massive military power in Iran or elsewhere
in the Gulf, would be deterred from such a move out of fear
of an American response. The Rapid Deployment Force
that the Carter Administration had been building up for use

in emergencies in the region was not scheduled to achieve
full strength until 1985. By then, the Kremlin, whose oil
production, according to Central Intelligence Agency estimates, will have leveled off, might be tempted to use its
military power in the Gulf to insure future supplies of foreign oil. If such a scenario were indeed to occur, the United
States might have no other option but to choose between
going along with such a move or resorting to full-scale
war—with all that implied.

It also remained to be seen whether the Carter Doctrine,
which was designed to protect the Gulf against external
agression, could prove effective against indigenous political
or nationalistic forces that threatened at any moment to
engulf the region in conflict or chaos. With the outbreak of
war between Iran and Iraq, the United States, which lacked
leverage with either country, was forced to the sidelines,
helpless to shape events and oblige the two sides to come to
the peace table. As a result of the fighting, some of the worst
fears of the United States had been realized by the cuts in oil
production in both countries. Only the existence of huge
stocks of oil in the West was what, for the while at least,
spared the world from a new round of rapidly escalating
petroleum prices.

The Carter Doctrine, assuming that it would be adopted
as policy by President Ronald Reagan, seemed less likely to
prove effective against local forces of subversion. Yet, there
was abundant evidence that internal subversion rather than
external attacks would likely be the major threat to stability
in the region. The attack by fanatical Muslims against the
Grand Mosque inMecca underscored this point. It was not
at all certain how durable the Saudi royal establishment
really was and whether it had the support of its people.
Ironically, the puritanical Saudi government has proved
vulnerable on its religious flank to fundamentalist elements
within the country who have contended that the government
was being led astray by corruption and forces of modernization.

The problems of the Persian Gulf, which the Carter Administration wrestled with during its second two years in office, are high on the agenda of President Reagan. With the release of the hostages, the Reagan Administration, it was speculated, might be able to deal with the manifold problems facing the United States in the region in ways that President Carter could not. The long-standing goals of the United States in the Gulf—peace and stability—will not change, albeit the means for promoting them may be altered by the new president. President Reagan might well decide, after careful review of the situation, that the interests of his country might be better served by placing a greater emphasis on diplomacy than on military power. In the final analysis, Washington faced a need of coming to terms with the Iranian revolution and what this means in terms of Iran's future.

THIS BOOK DEALS WITH A NUMBER of the main issues confronting the United States—and the West—in the area extending westward from Pakistan to the Arabian peninsula. As one crisis after another broke out in Iran, Pakistan, the Yemens and Afghanistan, the region became identified in the minds of many Americans as the "arc of crisis." In the succeeding chapters, these crises are presented mainly in terms of their impact on the United States. This discussion also deals with the role of the Soviet Union in each of the countries and the impact that its activities have had on the United States. The picture that emerges indicates that detente between the two superpowers has, to a considerable extent, been eroded by what has happened in these Third World countries.

MURRAY GORDON

Vienna, Austria
November, 1980

'Arc of Crisis':
Threat to U.S. Interests

Like a siege, political instability toward the end of the 1970s laid hold on United States interests in an arc of countries extending from Pakistan to Ethiopia.

In Iran and Ethiopia, governments long friendly to Washington, were overthrown by revolutionary forces hostile to American interests. In Turkey, Pakistan and Saudi Arabia, countries which had close political and economic ties with the U.S., relations cooled or became problematic.

The Soviet military intervention in Afghanistan, coming in 1979 at a time of growing political disintegration and economic chaos in Iran, created, in the view of some disinterested political observers, a new strategic balance in the region that directly threatened U.S. interests in the Persian Gulf. The Kremlin's military venture outside its traditionally acknowledged satellite sphere of influence in Eastern Europe precipitated a major crisis in relations with the United States.

It was against this background that President Jimmy Carter declared in his State of the Union address to a joint session of Congress January 23, 1980 that Soviet forces in Afghanistan posed a "grave threat" to the Middle East oil fields and that the United States would use "any means necessary, including military force," to repel an attack on the Persian Gulf.

What gave added urgency to the situation in the Gulf area was the large Soviet military presence in the People's Democratic Republic of Yemen (PDRY), or Southern Yemen, and in Ethiopia.

This vast region, embracing the Persian Gulf, the Arabian Peninsula and the Horn of Africa, is of great strategic importance to both the United States and the Soviet Union; it gave promise of becoming the world's cockpit of the early 1980s.

There are four overarching factors that make this overwhelmingly Islamic region so important in world affairs and an arena of acute rivalry between the superpowers:

Its subsoil holds about three-fourths of the proven and estimated world oil reserves upon which the Western world and Japan are dependent for their economic survival. Saudi Arabia, Iran and the other oil-producing states of the Gulf area account for about two-thirds of the total production of the Organization of Petroleum Exporting Countries (OPEC).

The region lies directly adjacent to the Soviet Union. Anything of major importance that occurs in such countries as Turkey, Iran or Afghanistan is almost certain to be of direct concern to Moscow. The Kremlin's decision to send troops into Afghanistan, it has been argued, may have been prompted by the possible effect that the growing instability in this Marxist country could have on the Soviet Union.

The region, moreover, is the locus of one of the most intractable conflicts of the twentieth century: Zionism versus Arab nationalism. It was generally recognized that in the event of another Arab-Israel war, its effects would directly and almost immediately be felt in the Persian Gulf and Arabian Peninsula. And given the stake of the U.S. and the

Soviet Union in the outcome of such a conflict, it could very well lead to a confrontation between them.

Finally, the region is the birthplace of Judaism, Christianity and Islam. This fact alone forever insures the intrusion of religious passions into the area.

Ebbing American Influence in the Region

For the United States, long the beneficiary of the political *status quo* in the region, developments there since 1978 have posed a serious threat to its strategic interests. In the unremitting struggle for power and influence between Washington and Moscow, the position of the United States has declined in a number of key countries in the region while that of its rival has, on balance, improved.

This was as much as acknowledged by President Carter's National Security Adviser Zbigniew Brzezinski in a speech before the Foreign Policy Association in December 1978. Painting a somber picture of events unfolding in the region as they affected American interests, Brzezinski stated: "An arc of crisis stretches along the shores of the Indian Ocean, with fragile social and political structures in a region of vital importance to us threated by fragmentation. The resulting political chaos could well be filled by elements hostile to our values and sympathetic to our adversaries." These references to an "arc of crisis," which captured widespread public attention in the U.S. and abroad, were made at a time when in Iran the shah's throne hung in the balance, rioting wracked a number of Turkey's eastern provinces, the Soviets were consolidating their position in Ethiopia as a result of the military defeat of Somalia by Cuban-backed Ethiopian troops, and the Egyptian-Israeli peace talks were at an impasse.

Viewing the same political developments, Henry A. Kissinger spoke in even more forthright language, warning that unless Washington acted decisively to restrain Soviet expansionism in the region to prove to the Kremlin "that a relaxa-

tion of tensions is not compatible with a systematic attempt
to overturn the geopolitical equilibrium," then "sooner or
later a showdown is likely to occur with tremendous changes
for everybody." The former Secretary of State expressed
concern that the sweep of events could cause countries like
Turkey, Iran, Pakistan and Saudi Arabia to stray from their
"clear-cut foreign policy orientation" to something "much
more ambiguous," creating an "area of enormous uncer-
tainty."

Picking up this theme, *The Economist* (London), in a
widely noted article titled "The Crumbling Triangle"
(December 8, 1978), wrote that the failure of the American
people, traumatized by the Vietnam war, to counter the
Russian-Cuban operation in Angola in 1975 "led to the
Soviet-Cuban success in Ethiopia ... which, in conjunction
with the turmoil in Iran and the coups in Kabul and Aden, is
now having its effect on the political complexion of the
whole triangle." Within the triangular area extending from
Kabul to Ankara to Addis Ababa, warned *The Economist*,
"former neutral may become pro-Russian" and "some
former pro-westerners nervously neutral."

Until the end of 1977, the overall position of the United
States in this vast region had not been a source of concern.
The shah, long-time ally of the U.S., appeared solidly
entrenched, and the flow of oil from Iran and the other
Persian Gulf states continued without interruption. Soviet
influence in the region remained limited and, except for
military facilities it had acquired in Southern Yemen and
Somalia, there was no significant Russian military presence
in the region. President Anwar al-Sadat's decision to expel
the approximately 15,000 Soviet military advisers from
Egypt in 1972 and to cancel the Egyptian-Soviet friendship
treaty in 1976 proved to be a severe setback for Moscow's
Middle East policy from which it had not recovered. Following the 1973 Yom Kippur war, Washington seized the
initiative for promoting peace between Israel and certain of
the Arab countries and kept the Soviets outside this process.

Containing Soviet Influence

The United States had built up its position in the region following World War II through a combination of vigorous diplomacy, covert intelligence activities and the extension of economic and military assistance to friendly governments. Washington, in the post-war era, established good ties with Iran, Turkey, Ethiopia and Pakistan. And although the United States actively supported the creation of Israel in 1947, this did not prevent it from developing normal political and economic relations with most Arab countries.

The United States became involved in Persian Gulf affairs right after World War II in response to Soviet attempts to dismember Iran. In 1946, the Truman Administration reacted strongly in thwarting Stalin's attempts to establish puppet states in Iranian Azerbaijan and Kurdestan. Through this forceful intervention, the United States demonstrated a commitment to the independence and territorial integrity of Iran. American ascendancy was assured when, in 1953, the Central Intelligence Agency clandestinely acted to restore to his throne the young Shah Mohammed Riza Pahlevi, who had been forced to flee the country.

Until he was deposed in January 1979, the shah remained a close friend of the U.S. and the West, and the relationship proved mutually beneficial. Iran became a member of the Central Treaty Organization (CENTO), an American-conceived defensive pact that was designed to block Russian expansion into the Middle East and deny it access to the Indian Ocean. With Washington's blessing, the shah assumed the role of protector of the Persian Gulf. In 1971, President Nixon agreed to sell Iran virtually unlimited amounts of weapons to strengthen it as the leading military power in the Gulf region.

In circumstances not too dissimilar from those involving Iran, the U.S. had also developed close ties with Turkey. The coincidence of interests between the two countries grew out of communist activity in Greece and threats of Soviet expansionism in Iran following hard on the end of World War II. In neighboring Greece, communist guerrillas, abetted by Moscow, were fighting to win control of the government; with the support of Yugoslavia and Albania, then in the Russian fold, the guerrillas came close to taking over Athens in 1946. These developments coincided with Moscow's attempts to promote "People's Republics" in Iranian Kurdestan and Azerbaijan. This pincer-like movement from Greece and Iran, linked with Soviet demands for the retrocession of the Kars region of Turkey (which had been Russian territory from 1878 to 1920) and the establishment of a "joint defense" arrangement for the Bosphorus and Dardanelles, caused Ankara to look to the United States for political and military support.

In Washington, the communist threats to Greece, Turkey and Iran were seen as an extension of Soviet expansionism in Eastern Europe. When the British government announced in 1947 that it could no longer carry the economic burden of assisting Greece and Turkey, the United States stepped into the breach. In a message to Congress, President Harry S. Truman set forth a plan of his own—known as the Truman Doctrine—to provide economic and military assistance to these two beleaguered countries. This doctrine became the first clear-cut statement of U.S. policy to contain Soviet expansionism. In 1952, three years after NATO was founded, the United States sponsored Turkey and Greece as full members of the Atlantic Alliance.

In the early 1950s, President Dwight D. Eisenhower was anxious to extend the containment policy into the Middle East. Although American policy makers could only guess whether the Soviets had a long-range blueprint for control of the region, they were deeply concerned over the near term implications of Soviet activities there.

Since czarist times, the rulers of Russia have probed southward seeking access to the southern sea lanes that are now major oil routes and thus a lifeline of the industrialized world. Until now, the Western powers have succeeded in thwarting the Russians. In the nineteenth century, the British Empire, from such places as the Ottoman Empire, Persia and the Northwest Frontier of India, intrigued and battled against Russian expansion. Rudyard Kipling called this struggle "the great game." In the twentieth century the game has continued, with somewhat different rules and different players. The Soviets have replaced the czars, and the U.S. has supplanted Britain. The stakes have also changed. Instead of seeking only warm-water ports, the Soviets are attempting to control access to the oil riches of the Middle East and the Persian Gulf.

Initial American efforts to block Soviet expansion into the region through a Middle East defense pact foundered on the Arab-Israel conflict. Egypt, the major Arab power, was suspicious of American motives. President Gamal Abdel Nasser was encountering difficulties in securing American financial support for the construction of the Aswan Dam, and, as it later developed, he had been contemplating approaching Moscow for the necessary resources for this mammoth venture. The Egyptian president was also fearful that the proposed pact could serve as the basis for U.S. hegemony in the Middle East. After negotiating the termination of the British presence in the Suez Canal zone not long after the military seized power in 1952, the increasingly anti-Western Egyptian leader opposed the reintroduction of British, American or other Western military forces under the cloak of an anti-communist defense pact.

By 1955, Secretary of State John Foster Dulles, architect of Soviet containment policy and its staunchest supporter during most of the Eisenhower Administration, abandoned the idea of forming such a pact around a nucleus of Arab states. He then devised the "Northern Tier" concept for the defense of the region. Under this approach, an alliance was formed of countries situated along the southern flank of the Soviet Union. Dulles envisioned this grouping as a Southwest Asian counterpart of NATO. Its purpose was to blunt Soviet attempts to penetrate the Arab Middle East and block Moscow from realizing an age-old Russian ambition of reaching warm-water ports in the Arabian Sea. The original members of the alliance were Turkey, Iran, Iraq, Pakistan and Great Britain; the United States limited itself to associate-member status. After a leftist military coup in Iraq in 1958 overthrew the pro-Western monarchy, the new Iraqi government opted out of the alliance, which, until then, had been known as the Baghdad Pact. Its headquarters then moved from the Iraqi capital to Ankara, and the scaled-down alliance was renamed the Central Treaty Organization (CENTO).

Turkey's membership in both NATO and CENTO established, in theory, an interlocking relationship between the two alliances. A similar situation presumably obtained between CENTO and the South East Asian Treaty Organization (SEATO) through Pakistan. A member of both alliances, the latter could, if attacked, invoke the collective security arrangements of both treaties. Although the United States undoubtedly viewed these interlocking arrangements as an important way of strengthening the anti-communist coalition that it was forging in large sections of the world, it was doubtful whether things would have worked out that way. The NATO countries had all along viewed the provisions of their agreement as limited to Western Europe; the major Western colonial powers, England and France, having just given up their empires in the Middle East and Asia, had no compelling national interest in sending troops to these areas. And, as for Pakistan, which enjoyed the protective shields of both CENTO and SEATO, it subsequently discovered that neither pact proved of any value during any of its three wars with neighboring India.

Apart from these collective security accords, the United States, in line with its policy of containing Soviet expansionism, signed a number of bilateral agreements with several of the countries in the area touching on their security needs. Washington, even before the creation of NATO, had implicitly agreed to come to Turkey's defense under the Truman Doctrine. Pakistan, too, had developed close ties with the United States. In 1959 President Eisenhower signed an executive agreement pledging U.S. military support for Pakistan in the event it was attacked. The agreement and the collective security arrangements laid the political groundwork for Pakistan to receive massive quantities of military assistance from the United States.

Far to the west, in the Horn of Africa, the United States actively courted Emperor Haile Selassie, the venerable leader of Ethiopia. Starting in 1953, Washington had supplied Ethiopia with three hundred million dollars worth of arms, and, in return, was allowed to maintain a communications base in Kagnew, Asmara. From Washington's vantage point, a strong pro-Western Ethiopia would have a stabilizing effect in the Red Sea. This waterway was a major sea route for tankers carrying Persian Gulf oil through the Suez Canal to Western Europe. The Red Sea was also of vital importance to Israel. President Eisenhower had given Jerusalem a pledge that it would have assured access to the Red Sea in return for Israeli withdrawal from the Sinai Peninsula and Gaza Strip following the 1956 Suez-Sinai war. These were among the more important reasons why the United States promoted friendly ties with Addis Ababa, which, with American (and later Israeli) aid, had become a formidable Red Sea power.

U.S. Interest in the Gulf

For more than a quarter of a century, the security of the Persian Gulf had been a major concern of American foreign policy. Until 1968, when the British government announced that it was giving up its military presence East of Suez, responsibility for the region's security fell to the British, with the United States maintaining a supportive role. Since then, the United States has commited itself to the defense of the

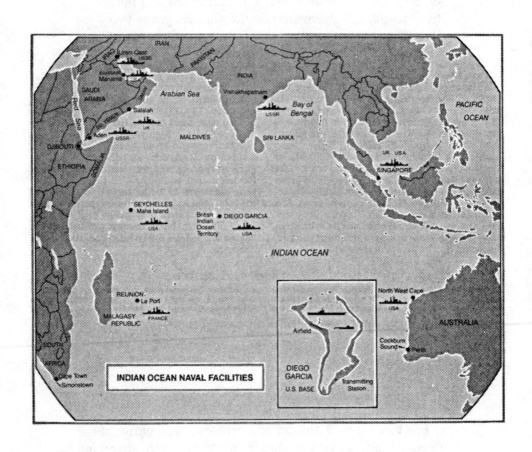

INDIAN OCEAN NAVAL FACILITIES

DIEGO GARCIA
U.S. BASE

region. The actual task of protecting the Gulf was assumed by the shah of Iran under an arrangement worked out with the United States.

By undertaking responsibility for the defense of the Gulf, the United States was able to secure several interests that were important to the preservation of its own national interests and those of its Western allies. Foremost among these was maintaining assured access to the oil riches of the regions.

The oil-producing states in the region cover about half of the West's requirements, and their vast reserves will remain indispensable in meeting future needs until alternative energy sources become available. Production of Saudi Arabia, Iran, Iraq, Kuwait and the United Arab Emirates runs to about twenty million barrels a day (before the overthrow of the shah), or two-thirds of the Organization of Petroleum Exporting Countries' daily output of thirty million barrels. OPEC production is slightly more than half of total world oil production. Any threat to this oil supply, particularly at a time of a tight balance between supply and demand, could threaten the economies of the Western nations.

The United States, despite its considerable oil production, has become increasingly dependent on foreign sources of oil, particularly those of the Middle East and Persian Gulf. Despite the high pitched rhetoric of the Nixon, Ford and Carter Administrations for greater self-sufficiency in oil, the reverse has actually occurred. American oil dependence has grown since the Arab oil embargo of 1973. That year, the United States imported 2.4 million barrels of oil per day from Arab producers. Six years later, the figure had doubled, with the United States importing 4.9 million barrels a day.

The oil-producing Arab states in the Persian Gulf and Iran had gradually become important markets for American goods and services. Following the quadrupling of oil prices in 1973, these countries have been acquiring the money to expand imports on a huge scale. As a result, they have become the fastest growing market in the world for American exports. These trade relations figure importantly in total American exports and are a vital factor in strengthening the overall U.S. balance of accounts. The import side of the trade ledger has received wide publicity as U.S. demand for Middle Eastern and Persian Gulf oil has risen. On the other hand, U.S. sales to the area have risen substantially. Whereas exports to the region were 3.5 billion dollars in 1973 and accounted for five per cent of total U.S. foreign trade, the dollar value of these exports rose to 12.3 billion dollars by 1977, or approximately ten per cent of all foreign sales.

The drive to expand the Middle East and Persian Gulf as markets for U.S. goods and services touched directly on America's economic and defense interests. The quantum leap in oil prices in 1973 created for the United States, and for much of the world as well, vast new monetary problems. On the one hand there was a need to develop financial mechanisms that would allow the recycling of the vast sums of money being accumulated by the oil producing countries into the international monetary system. There was a growing fear at the time, which subsequently proved unfounded, that Saudi Arabia and the other oil-rich states would, through their huge dollar reserves, acquire large stakes in American corporations; no less of a concern was the potential threat these countries posed to the stability of the international monetary system and to the dollar, on which this system is based.

A major component of U.S. trade has been armaments. The United States had emerged by 1975 as the most important of the twenty-eight states supplying weapons and military services to countries in the Persian Gulf. While Washington has been responsible in recent decades for well over fifty per cent of the worldwide arms trade, Persian Gulf states have accounted for as much as sixty per cent of munitions orders over the years. Between 1972 and 1978, Iran ordered 19.5 billion dollars worth of arms. One Congressman has referred to this as "the most rapid buildup of

military power under peacetime conditions of any nation in
the history of the world." Saudi Arabia's record in arms
acquisition in the same period, although not nearly as great,
was impressive nonetheless.

For the United States, the massive sales of armaments,
increasingly of the most sophisticated variety, had multiple
purposes. One, as already noted, was economic. The sale of
costly weapons helped improve the negative balance of trade
that was directly attributable to the spiraling cost of oil.
Another consideration, not often mentioned, was to lighten
the heavy burden of weapons development. The research
and development costs of sophisticated weapons technology
is a strain on the resources of even a country like the United
States. Large cost overruns, which are virtually inevitable in
a period of accelerating inflation, often make it difficult for
the Pentagon to convince a budget-minded Congress of the
feasibility of a particular weapons system. By selling substantial numbers of planes, for example, to Iran, Israel,
Saudi Arabia and other countries, the Defense Department
is able to spread the research and development costs and
reduce the unit cost of each plane.

The armaments business has entailed considerations that
obviously transcend economic concerns alone. To the extent
that it sells sophisticated weapons to a country, the United
States is often in a position to enhance its political and
military influence there. The sale of such arms to Iran,
Kuwait and Saudi Arabia required the deployment of a vast
army of experts and technicians to help their military establishments to use and maintain them. Overall, their presence
helped contribute to continued cooperation between Washington and the countries dependent on such assistance.

There are, of course, negative side-effects to the massive
sale of armaments to the countries in the Gulf and elsewhere
in the region; they will be reviewed in greater detail later on.
It would be useful to point some of these out to indicate that
U.S. arms policies in the region have not been an unmixed
blessing.

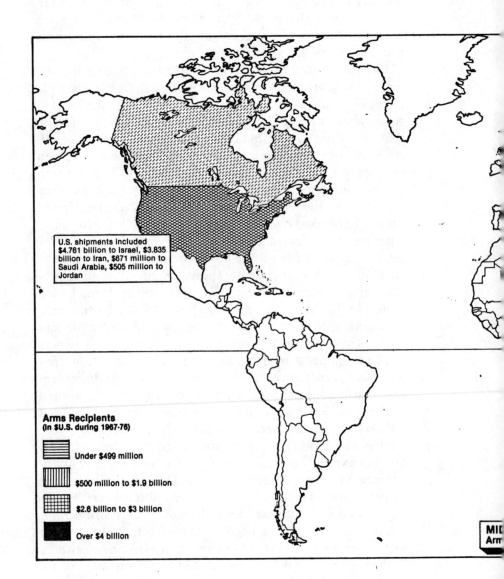

U.S. shipments included
$4.761 billion to Israel, $3.835
billion to Iran, $671 million to
Saudi Arabia, $505 million to
Jordan

Arms Recipients
(In $U.S. during 1967-76)

Under $499 million

$500 million to $1.9 billion

$2.6 billion to $3 billion

Over $4 billion

MII
Arm

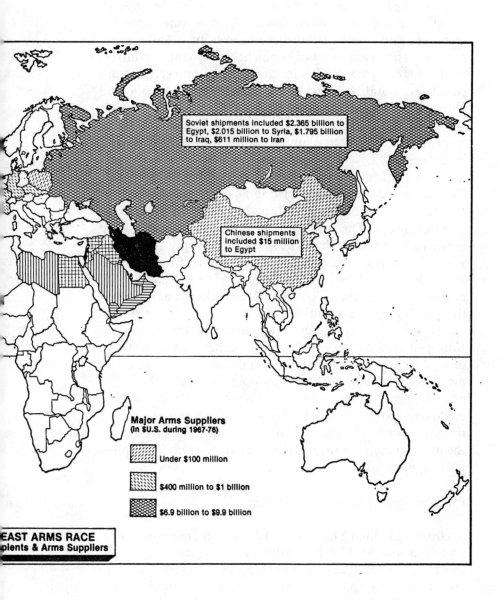

Soviet shipments included $2.365 billion to Egypt, $2.015 billion to Syria, $1.795 billion to Iraq, $611 million to Iran

Chinese shipments included $15 million to Egypt

Major Arms Suppliers
(In $U.S. during 1967-76)

Under $100 million

$400 million to $1 billion

$6.9 billion to $9.9 billion

EAST ARMS RACE
plents & Arms Suppliers

Vast expenditures on armaments even in the oil-rich countries have been a heavy burden by diverting necessary resources and limited trained manpower away from development. The availability of sophisticated weapons contributed to the growth of an arms race between certain countries, notably between Iran and Saudi Arabia and between Iran and Iraq. More than that, it can be argued, access to these arms had the effect of intensifying rival territorial and dynastic claims among some of the countries in the region.

The transfer of weapons to Pakistan, while viewed by the Carter Administration as one possible response to the Soviet invasion of Afghanistan, could be considered to threaten India. The latter country has traditionally been sensitive to attempts by Washington to supply Islamabad with armaments as part of a policy to contain Soviet expansion. Delhi has feared that a strengthened Pakistan could embolden it to reclaim Kashmir. It can also be argued that the shah's imperial ambitions in the Gulf and in the Indian Ocean were fed by the growing power of his American-equipped armed forces. These developments ran counter to official U.S. policy of promoting stability in the region. Far more serious from the American point of view is the possibility of being drawn into a local or regional conflict. This could come about by the continuing dependence of many of these states on American civilian and military personnel in the use and maintenance of their growing arsenal of sophisticated weapons.

U.S. Policy in Defense of the Gulf

Growing United States and Western dependence on Persian Gulf and Middle East oil, and the compelling need to assure continued access to the region's vast oil reserves in an era of growing rivalry for this precious commodity, had prompted Washington to be concerned over the security of the Gulf. U.S. policies dating back to the end of World War ll supportive of Iran's territorial integrity were an implicit commitment to the defense of the Gulf.

Until the mid-1960s, there was little real concern that the security of the Gulf was in jeopardy from either external or internal sources. Overall, the defense of the region was in the hands of the British, whose small naval force was more than adequate to deal with any local threat to the peace. Past Iraqi threats to Kuwait did not get far because of the presence of the British fleet. The Soviet Union, the sole potential threat to the region, did not manifest any aggressive designs on the region; in the early 1960s, the Kremlin had worked out a *modus vivendi* with the shah that appeared to rule out possible trouble from the Russian side of the border. In the 'fifties and 'sixties, the Soviet fleet was of modest proportions and was no match for the American Navy. Moscow, moreover, as an exporter of oil, had little interest in the crude oil of the Gulf. And as far as oil production in the region was concerned, this remained firmly in the hands of the Western oil companies. Once these companies worked out terms covering royalties and taxes with the governments for a particular time period, the governments showed no disposition to become involved in the production, distribution and sale of oil.

The region, despite territorial differences between a number of the countries, itself was remarkably free of conflict. There was a pronounced tendency to resolve outstanding disputes through peaceful means. The 1975 agreement between Iran and Iraq to resolve differences over the Shatt al Arab and Teheran's support of the Kurdish revolt in Iraq were examples of the willingness of the Persian Gulf states to resort to diplomatic means to avoid conflict. The Gulf, moreover, was shielded from the most serious threat to the peace in the region: the Arab-Israel conflict. Although sympathetic to the Palestinian cause, the Arab states in the Gulf were not disposed to become participants in this seemingly intractable struggle. The shah, for reasons of his own, maintained good relations with Israel.

Beginning around the mid-1960s, the security of the Gulf was beginning to become a matter of major concern for the shah, and later for the United States. The monarch's growing disillusionment with CENTO and the threat he perceived originating from Iraq prompted him to take a strong interest in the security of the Gulf. While the shah held that the treaty provided some kind of guarantee against a serious Soviet threat, it was said that he felt it would be of little benefit in protecting the country in local conflict. This, he apparently felt, Iran would have to deal with through its own military power which, at that time, was meager. His decision to discount CENTO as a protective shield was a consequence of the failure of any of the contracting powers to come to Pakistan's assistance in 1965 at the time of its war with India. The implications of this were not lost on him in the event of a conflict with Iraq or any other country in the region.

There were, from the shah's point of view, two serious threats to Iran's suzerainity in the Gulf during the 1960s. One emananted from Iraq and the other from Egypt. Oil, in both instances, was the root cause. For Iran, the Gulf was important both as a source of oil and as the only available channel for its export. Two important changes in the country's oil industry made it more important than ever for the government to become involved in assuring security in the Gulf. The first of these was the development of the off-shore oilfields; the beginning of such explorations in Iranian water had taken place in 1957. The second major factor was the construction of the immense oil terminal on Kharg Island, an Iranian possession some thirty miles from the mainland. This port had been developed at tremendous cost because the oil terminal at Abadan suffered from two serious defects: the shallowness of the approach channel—the Shatt al Arab—restricted use of the port; compounding this problem was the fact that the approaches to the port were under the control of Iraq. The Shatt al Arab, jointly shared by Iraq and Iran, is the waterway where the Tigris and Euphrates rivers empty into the Persian Gulf. Until the agreement between the two countries in 1975, Iraq's border had extended to the Iranian side of the Shatt al Arab. As a result, Iranian ships, notably oil tankers, had to pass through Iraqi-controlled waters. To the shah, who was bent on making Iran the primary power in the Gulf, this was an intolerable situation.

In Iraq, the ruling Ba'athist party had pursued policies that placed it at serious odds with Teheran. The republican and revolutionary cast of the government, which could not have differed more from Iran's monarchical and conservative rule, vigorously espoused socialism. This was perceived as a very real threat not only by Iran but to the other states in the Gulf, which were ruled by monarchs of one form or other. Baghdad, moreover, had established close ties with the Soviet Union, with which it had signed a treaty of friendship. Its decision to renounce its membership in CENTO had complicated, as far as the shah was concerned, the problems of defending the region against external threats. The shah's policies in the Gulf had done much to heighten tensions with Iraq, thereby contributing to the very security problem within the region that he had sought to prevent. His claims in the Shatt al Arab, his ambitions in the Gulf and support of the Kurdish revolt within Iraq had exacerbated ties between the two countries.

The threat emanating from Egypt was more of a concern to the shah. Whereas Iraq was militarily weak and its armed forces were no match for the Iranian military establishment, Egypt under President Gamal Abdel Nasser had become a formidable military power. Like the Iraqis, Nasser had established close ties with the Soviets, from whom he received arms. There was no minimizing Nasser's charismatic appeal to the vast majority of Arabs in the Middle East and Persian Gulf. It was no secret that he coveted the oilfields of Iran, which are located in the largely Arab-inhabited southern province of Khuzistan. Publicly, Nasser referred to the Persian Gulf as the Arab Gulf, a point that was not lost on the Persian monarch who considered this vital waterway as an Iranian "lake."

Far more serious than the continuing barrage of propaganda emanating from Cairo was Nasser's policies in the Arabian peninsula as they began to unfold in the early and mid-1960s. As part of his pan-Arab policy, the Egyptian leader had sent a large expeditionary force to Yemen in 1962 to assist the republican revolutionary forces which had toppled the imam. The prolonged presence of these Egyptian forces in the Arabian peninsula, coupled with growing possibility of a British withdrawal from Aden, raised in Teheran the spectre of an irresistable Nasserist tide sweeping across the southern fringes of the peninsula and the establishment of a base from which to radicalize Muscat and Oman and threaten the conservative Arab countries situated along the Persian Gulf littoral. If this threat were to materialize, policy makers in Teheran held, Nasser would then be in a position to achieve his goal of dominating the Persian Gulf. Sharing Iran's concerns over Nasser was the Saudi Arabian government. Riyadh had been a constant supporter of the Yemeni royalists who had fought the Egyptian army to a standstill in the peninsula.

Developments in the eastern Mediterranean were to alter drastically the stalemated situation in the Yemen. Nasser's action of proclaiming a blockade of Eilat, Israel's southern port and gateway to Asia and Africa, led Egypt into a disastrous war with the Jewish state in June 1967. This forced Nasser to withdraw his army from Yemen and turn to the task of rebuilding his shattered military establishment and recovering the Sinai, which was lost to the victorious Israeli army.

These threats to the Gulf from Iraq and Egypt, the shah's failing confidence in CENTO and the imminent withdrawal of British forces East of Suez prompted Iran to embark upon a policy of becoming the foremost military power in the region. To make good in this aim, the shah undertook what was to become a vast armaments program. Starting in

1968, Teheran ordered large numbers of warplanes from the United States, including the sophisticated F-14; a major effort got under way to make Iran's modest navy the most formidable fleet in the Gulf; and the army was expanded to make it more than a match for any other in the region.

Diplomatically, the shah took a number of steps to improve relations with Saudi Arabia and the Lower Gulf states. Iran, Saudi Arabia and several of the Lower Gulf states negotiated demarcation agreements in which their respective offshore boundaries were recognized for the first time. The shah, in addition, relinquished Iran's long-standing claim to Bahrain. In doing this, he removed the seeds of potential conflict that had long bedevilled Arab-Iranian relations not only in Bahrain but elsewhere in the Gulf, notably in Saudi Arabia and Kuwait. And to improve his image within the Gulf Emirates, the shah extended economic aid to some of the poorer sheikhdoms.

Diplomacy was not always the path pursued by the shah, particularly where this involved efforts to extend his control over the Gulf. In 1969, he raised the dispute with Iraq over the Shatt al Arab to crisis level by declaring the 1937 treaty governing navigation rights on the waterway null and void. Iranian gunboats were dispatched up the Shatt and plied these waters at will despite strong protests from Baghdad. He also sent his marines to seize three Arab-owned islands at the mouth of the Gulf which, he feared, might be used by terrorist groups to hinder traffic in and out of the Gulf. As if to demonstrate Britain's military weakness in the region, the action took place shortly before London relinquished its protective role in November 1971. The timing created an altogether different impression in some Arab countries, where it was believed that the shah was in collusion with the British in the matter. Iraq, as a result, severed diplomatic ties with Iran and Britain, and Libya expropriated the assets of the British Petroleum company in the country; the Lower Gulf states experienced the worst scenes of violence and civil disorder since the 1967 Arab-Israel war, and communal

tensions between Arabs and Iranians increased. The irony of
it all was that Iran's professed reason for seizing the islands,
which was to insure stability and peace in the region, rang
somewhat hollow.

The key development that prompted the shah to become a
major factor in the security of the Gulf was Britain's decision
in 1968 to withdraw the last of its troops from the Far East
and the Persian Gulf by the end of 1971. This provided the
restless and politically ambitious ruler with the opportunity
he eagerly sought. In this respect, he received strong encouragement from the U.S., which feared that, unless steps were
taken before the British withdrawal, a dangerous military
vacuum would be created in the Gulf. The Russians, it was
argued, might be moved to fill this vacuum and jeopardize
Western access to the region's oil riches. In 1969, President
Nixon agreed to assign a key role to Iran in the defense of the
Gulf. To give substance to this strategy, the United States
undertook to build up Iran as a major regional military
power. In exchange for Iran's serving as "the guardian and
protector" of the Gulf, the Nixon Administration extended
a virtual *carte blanche* to the shah to purchase almost any
weapons system in the American arsenal. In 1972, the President and Secretary of State Henry Kissinger flew to Teheran
to seal the new U.S.-Iranian partnership. This understanding became the basis for the close political relations between
the two countries which was to last until the shah was forced
to flee Iran in January 1979. And as long as it endured, it
served U.S. and Western interests well. Successive administrations in Washington took at face value the shah's assump-
tions that the understanding also responded to the real
interests of Iran.

The decision to arm Iran was a corollary that followed the
so-called "Nixon Doctrine." First set forth during the Vietnam War, the doctrine provided the rationale for arming the
South Vietnamese army so that it could take over responsibility from American troops for defending South Vietnam.
This allowed President Nixon to fulfill his election cam-

paign pledge to put an end to U.S. involvement in this unpopular war. Applied to the Persian Gulf, the doctrine became the rationale for arming Iran to assume a role adjudged critical for the defense of U.S. interests in the region. Had the Nixon Administration attempted to involve the United States directly in the region, it would have encountered strong resistance in the country and from Congress. The Vietnam War had been a traumatic experience for the American people, and they were in no mood for new foreign ventures. At the time, the Persian Gulf was not seen as having strategic importance to the United States. There was a general lack of awareness of the growing U.S. dependence on foreign oil; the very notion of an "energy crisis" was only barely beginning to appear in the American political vocabulary and even less so in the public mind.

Within this set of political circumstances, the shah became a key figure in American strategic planning for the defense of the Persian Gulf. Iran, it was agreed, could purchase the weapons it deemed necessary for carrying out what for the United States was a surrogate role. With the quantum rise in oil prices following the 1973 Yom Kippur war, the shah acquired the means to accomplish what he was set on doing: become the "guardian and protector" of the Persian Gulf. As for Washington's part in this arrangement, it was prepared to sell unlimited quantities of arms, which became the visible symbol of its commitment to the shah.

The shah's overthrow put an end to this arrangement and, more fundamentally, dealt a shattering blow to U.S. interests in the region. The shah was the mainstay of American influence and power in the area; whether intended or not, the American strategic edifice in the Gulf had been built around one person.

Although the downfall of the shah and the establishment of an Islamic republic in Iran were indisputably major events in creating the crisis confronting the United States in the Persian Gulf, there were earlier indications that its position in the region was unraveling. This was due to a combi-

nation of factors: American losses in Iran and other friendly
nations; Soviet gains in such countries as Ethiopia, Southern Yemen and, most recently, Afghanistan. Washington's
inability to prevent the shah's overthrow and its failure to
counter the Kremlin's move into Ethiopia raised serious
questions in Saudi Arabia and in other pro-Western circles
within the region as to Washington's ability to contain
communist expansionism, and its reliability in defence of its
allies and friends in time of crisis. The Soviet record in
revolutionary Ethiopia and its growing naval presence in the
Indian Ocean provide vivid demonstrations of the Kremlin's
ability to project military power into the region. At the
regional level, the American-inspired system of alliances to
contain communist expansionism had lost much of its credibility. CENTO had become a tattered alliance. Serious
strains had developed between the United States and the two
other partners to the treaty—Turkey and Pakistan. Ankara's invasion of Cyprus in 1974 had created a deep rift with
Washington and alienated powerful political forces in Congress, which for a long time managed to keep an embargo on
the sale of arms to this NATO and CENTO ally. As for
Pakistan, its decision to go ahead to build an atomic bomb
caused the U.S. to cut off economic and military assistance
to the martial law government of President Zia ul-Haq.
Both countries, moreover, faced severe problems of civil
unrest. Martial law remained in effect in 13 of Turkey's
eastern provinces; and in Pakistan, the province of Baluchistan had been in a state of near insurrection for over seven
years. The fragility of established political as well as social
institutions in these and other countries in the region
friendly to the United States, or pro-Western in their political orientation, was another dimension to Washington's
problem of putting into effect a credible foreign policy that
could restore its influence in this strategic region.

Emerging Soviet Role in the Region

Soviet-U.S. Rivalry

The declining fortunes of the United States in the region have taken place against a background of solid, if not fitful, Soviet advances. In no small measure, these gains were the product of astute diplomacy, often employed in conjunction with military assistance programs. It has been this ability to convert their growing military power into political influence that has accounted for much of the success of the Soviets in Third World countries. This was the case in revolutionary Ethiopia, Angola and Southern Yemen.

In Ethiopia, the Kremlin had extended timely military aid to the beleaguered regime of Lieutenant Colonel Mengistu Haile Mariam at a critical moment in the conflict with Somalia in 1977-1978 over control of the Ogaden province. This aid, together with the powerful backing of Cuban troops, enabled the self-proclaimed Marxist government in Addis Ababa to repel the invading Somali soldiers from its eastern province. Since then, the Kremlin has held a preeminent position in the country, comparable to the role that the United States played during the heyday of Emperor Hailie Selassie's rule.

A not-too-dissimilar pattern of diplomatic *cum* military support for the Angolan nationalist movement of Dr. Agostinho Neto, the MPLA (Popular Movement for the Liberation of Angola), had enabled the Soviets to stake out a position of power in the country when it became independent in 1975.

A blend of diplomatic, economic and military support for the Marxist government in the People's Democratic Republic of Yemen (Southern Yemen) also explains the success of the Kremlin in gaining a foothold in this impoverished country situated in the southeast corner of the Arabian peninsula.

Soviet successes in the region can be attributed to several different but interrelated factors. Failure of U.S. policies in several key countries in the region accounts, to some extent, for these gains. To the extent that there are setbacks in U.S. policies, an opening is afforded to Moscow to exploit these targets of opportunity. This occurred in Ethiopia after the revolutionary government seized power and the Carter Administration proved unable to come to terms with it. The Kremlin was not long in taking advantage of the situation by responding to requests from Addis Ababa for large-scale military assistance to fend off the invading Somalis and suppress the growing secessionist movement in Eritrea. U.S. policies in Iran undoubtedly contributed to the growth of radicalism in the country and, as a result, led to the shah's overthrow. The monarch's mismanagement of industrial development and agrarian reform, his repressive policies towards dissenters and critics, failure to respond to popular demands for democratic institutions and his grandiose military ambitions were the chief causes of his undoing. When the end came for the Pahlevi regime in January 1979, the United States, which had been closely associated with various aspects of these policies, lost out. The system of military alliances that the United States had established in the region crumbled with the overthrow of its chief supporter and beneficiary.

It is not axiomatic that every U.S. strategic setback in the region results in an equivalent Soviet benefit. Conversely, not every Soviet setback generates a comparable American gain. There is no neat zero sum game operating behind every international move in the region. Nor is it that a superpower gain in a particular country is irreversible. Early gains for U.S. policy in Iran were certainly not permanent, and reverses, over the long run, may befall Moscow's policy in Afghanistan. The Kremlin's military intervention in this Islamic country may yet be a Soviet gain which turns out to be a Soviet loss. Moscow's well-entrenched position in Egypt is a case in point. In a bold move, President Sadat ordered Soviet advisers out of Egypt in 1972 and subsequently renounced the treaty of friendship with Russia that his predecessor had signed.

These developments, notwithstanding, there is some evidence that U.S. setbacks in the region, at least for the near and medium term, result in Soviet gains. That this occurs is due to the constellation of political forces that had been widespread in key countries until recently. By and large, U.S influence had been in the ascendancy, and Washington was the primary beneficiary of the *status quo*. Far-reaching political changes that pose a threat to the existing political order are likely to alter the *status quo* and prove detrimental to American and Western interests. This took place in Ethiopia, where a largely feudal but pro-Western monarchy was supplanted by a Marxist government oriented toward the Soviet Union. In Iran, a virulently anti-American, anti-Western government seized power from a regime that had served as a surrogate for U.S. interests in the Persian Gulf. There has existed a close ideological affinity between the People's Democratic Republic of Yemen and Ethiopia, on the one side, and with the Soviets, on the other. These two countries have been following the socialist model for economic development, thereby increasing their dependence on Moscow for economic assistance.

Gains and losses on the diplomatic checker board have not been the sole factor affecting the balance of superpower advantage in the region. No less significant has been the stability of the political, social and economic institutions in the countries in the region. The countries in the region that had been Washington's closest allies have suffered in one form or other from political instability and economic blight. The governments of the countries in the region have been authoritarian, barely concealing their lack of popular support. In Turkey, which until recently, at least, had been considered a democratic country, the fabric of government has severely eroded, finally resulting in a military take over in mid-1980. Not surprisingly, political opponents of the governments in power have increasingly resorted to violence to bring about change. The revolution in Iran came about, most observers agree, to answer the injustices of a corrupt and dictatorial government.

Turkey and Pakistan are examples of countries whose internal problems have had far-reaching effects on their capacity to play an effective role in foreign policy. In recent years, the relations of these two countries with the United States have suffered. In part, this has been due to divergent foreign policy matters. In the case of Turkey, relations were severely strained following Ankara's invasion of Cyprus in 1974 and its continuing military occupation of the northern part of this island state. This led to a U.S. embargo on the sale of arms to this NATO ally; in retaliation, Turkey closed about twenty-five American bases in 1975, most of them intelligence gathering facilities that monitored developments in the Soviet Union. Although the U.S. Congress revoked the embargo in September 1978, relations between the two countries have not fully recovered and are still dogged by the unresolved Cyprus issue.

More disturbing over the long run for Western interests in the region are Turkey's internal problems. The country has experienced severe political instability brought on by rampant inflation and a stagnant economy. Martial law, imposed in certain of the eastern provinces of the country at the end of 1978 as a result of riots in the province of Kahramanmaras, had failed to stem the wave of urban terrorism and political assassination. In the riots in Kahramanmaras, more than 100 people died in battles between Sunni and Alevi Muslim sects and their supporters of the radical right and left. These internal problems, coupled with events in neighboring Iran and the revival of Islamic fundamentalism within the region, led to a military take-over September 12, 1980 and raised questions as to whether Ankara can be counted on to stay within its traditional pro-Western foreign policy orbit.

United States relations with Pakistan, its closest ally on the Indian subcontinent, have also suffered. This has become more painful for the United States, which, following the Soviet invasion of Afghanistan, had hoped to strengthen Islamabad as a bulwark against Russian expansionism in southwest Asia. Prior to the Russian takeover in Kabul, ties between Washington and Pakistan had nosedived. In November 1978, a mob of Muslim fanatics had sacked the U.S. embassy in Islamabad. In April 1979, the Carter Administration, suspicious that the Pakistanis were developing nuclear weapons, cut off all economic aid to Pakistan. Since the early 1950s, Washington's program of aid to the country, one of its largest anywhere in the world, had totaled more than five billion dollars. Another source of strain between the two countries had been Washington's decision a few years earlier to turn down a Pakistani request to buy 100 A-7 fighter jets. The principal reason for this decision was the concern of India, which, having fought three wars with Pakistan, was not disposed to go along with any military buildup across its border.

Troublesome as these issues have been, there are other considerations relating to Pakistan's internal political situation that make any future role for it in the defense of the region problematic. Specifically, these have to do with the military regime ruling the country and the continued political unrest in Baluchistan, the largest (113,000 square miles) of Pakistan's four provinces. In 1977, a military junta led by General Mohammed Zia ul-Haq toppled the civilian government of President Zulfikar Ali Bhutto and returned the country to military rule. Despite early pledges by the martial law government to hold national elections, General Zia went back on his word. Commenting on these developments, the U.S. State Department, in its annual report to Congress on human rights conditions around the world, observed: "On October 16, 1979, President Zia indefinitely postponed national elections, dissolved all political parties, expanded the jurisdiction of military courts and imposed formal censorship of newspapers." Apart from the issue of restoring democracy at the national level, Zia refused to accede to the demands of the Baluchis for provincial self-rule. Large elements of the Pakistani army continued to stay on in the province, prepared to suppress any local efforts to renew the struggle for autonomy. Thus, General Zia had abandoned the two premises by which he sought to lend legitimacy to his coup: new elections and reconciliation with Baluchistan.

Reports from Pakistan indicated that General Zia's repressive policies had made his government increasingly unpopular. In early 1980, the government admitted that there had been an attempted coup that had been put down. The growing political instability in Islamabad had posed a serious problem to Carter Administration foreign policy strategists. Mindful of what following the overthrow of the unpopular government of the shah, there had been a certain wariness by the Administration to embrace a government which, by most indications, lacked the support of the people. There was also much reason to fear that the Zia regime would have taken fresh U.S. arms and used them against the Baluchis and other non-Punjabi minorities that it needed to

conciliate in order to strengthen and legitimize its rule.
Given these circumstances, a formal alliance, or even tacit
understanding with the Zia government could have proven a
disaster to the U.S.

Soviet Policies in the Region

It would be wrong to conclude that Soviet advances in the
regions are solely, or largely, due to U.S. diplomatic setbacks. There is strong evidence that many of its new-found
gains there are the direct result of a strategy of helping
Marxist parties to achieve political power in selected countries. Through such a strategem, it is said, the Kremlin
believed that it would be able to exercise desired political
influence within the country.

Between 1975 and the end of 1979, seven pro-Soviet communist parties have seized power in as many countries in
Asia and Africa. Indochina, during this period, came under
the domination of the People's Republic of Vietnam, which
has been closely allied to the Soviet Union. In the spring of
1975, North Vietnam, after years of war, gained control of
South Vietnam, and its puppet Pathet Lao movement seized
power in Laos. Four years later, Vietnamese troops crossed
over into Cambodia, driving out the pro-Chinese Pol Pot
regime and replacing it with one subservient to Hanoi.

In Africa, pro-Soviet communist parties have seized
power in Angola and Ethiopia. After a brief civil war in
Angola in 1975-1976, hard on the departure of the Portu-
gese, Agostinho Neto's Marxist-Leninist Popular Movement for the Liberation of Angola (MPLA) defeated two
rival factions with Soviet and Cuban military aid. In early
1977, in a "red terror" campaign directed against other
military leaders who had shared power with him following
the overthrow of Emperor Haile Selassie in 1974, Lieutenant Colonel Mengistu Haile Mariam and his group of communist military officers won control of the government in

Ethiopia. The Kremlin's decision to side with Ethiopia against Somalia, following the latter's invasion of the Ethiopian province of Ogaden, did cost the Soviets the friendship of the Somalis, who renounced their treaty of friendship with Moscow.

Across the Red Sea in South Yemen, the communist faction of the ruling coalition of leftists in South Yemen's government carried out a successful armed coup against President Salim Robaye Ali. And in Afghanistan in the spring of 1978, the People's Party led by Nur Mohammed Taraki staged an armed coup against the military government of President Mohammed Daoud. A year and a half later, Moscow, apparently dissatisfied with developments inside Afghanistan, sent troops into the country and installed a new leader whose subservience to the Kremlin was generally acknowledged.

There were other attempts to seize power through force that appear to have been aided by the Soviet Union—one in Somalia and the other in the Sudan. In Somalia, President Mohamed Siad Barre renounced his Treaty of Friendship with Moscow and expelled Soviet advisers in October 1977 in response to the Kremlin's decision to back the Marxist government in Ethiopia. On April 9, 1978, Barre announced that his government had foiled an attempted military coup taken in the interests of the "new imperialists," Barre's codeword for the Russians and Cubans. The following September, Somali military courts sentenced seventeen army officers to death and jailed twice that number for complicity in the coup attempt. In the Sudan, there were attempted coups against President Mohammed Gaafer el-Nimeiry in July 1976 and February 1977. The Sudanese leader charged that these attempts were "manipulated by foreign hands." As if to indicate whose hands were suspect, Khartoum, in May 1977, ousted the ninety Soviet military advisers in the country and requested that Moscow cut back on the size of its diplomatic mission.

The Soviet Union in the Third World

Before considering specific policies and actions of the Kremlin in the region, it would be helpful to understand Soviet attitudes toward political developments in Third World countries.

Moscow's interest in the Third World can be traced to the very birth of the Soviet state in October 1917. Lenin's expectation that the decolonialization process would revolutionize the international system was thoroughly realistic, although his ultimate hope that this development would contribute decisively to the collapse of the capitalist order has proved wrong. The decolonialization process, which was just beginning in earnest in Lenin's day, was beyond the power of the new Soviet state to shape or influence in any meaningful way. The Soviet leader quickly adjusted to the doctrinal and diplomatic demands of this situation and steered clear of any involvement in colonial independence movements. His successor, Stalin, adhered closely to this line. To Stalin, revolution was synonymous with Soviet state power, and whatever did not contribute directly to that power was inherently suspect. During the late twenties and the thirties, the Soviet dictator was absorbed with the task of transforming the Soviet Union into an industrial state and destroying everyone he believed to be his enemy. In foreign policy matters, Stalin was cautious in practice and extremely defensive in motivation. His overarching aim was to protect the emerging Soviet state from military threats arising in Europe and Japan. Even after the defeat of Nazi Germany, his politics remained continental in scope; nonetheless, his military victory over his archenemy and his political successes in eastern Europe clearly altered the Eurasian, and hence world, balance of power.

This foreign policy orientation began to change after Nikita S. Khrushchev came to power. The new Soviet leadership began to identify with the national liberation philosophy,

post-colonial nation-building process and the growing cry
of economic development that was beginning to be sounded
in the fifties in the fast-growing Third World. The Kremlin's
response was to provide limited amounts of economic aid to
selected countries, military assistance where this could
weaken Western influence; wherever it could, the Kremlin
sided with the growing national liberation movements in
their struggle against western colonial rule. This was a far
cry from the "socialism in one country" policy that had been
vigorously pursued by Lenin and Stalin. Of particular significance was Soviet willingness to cooperate with local nationalist leaders, who generally were neither workers nor
peasants. In the past, these nationalists had been condemned as reactionaries, who were serving the interests of
their own social and economic class. The Soviets held that
ultimately these national revolutions would be transformed
by "objective" economic forces into class revolutions. In any
event, it was argued that these revolutions would be self-
sustaining and would place little burden on the Soviet state.
Between 1954 and 1964, Soviet economic credits and grants
to non-communist Third World countries totaled about
four billion dollars, of which only 1.5 billion dollars was
actually drawn. By the end of 1964, Soviet military assistance, mostly in the form of long-term credits, had been
extended to approximately fifteen countries, but at a total
volume of approximately three billion dollars. By contrast,
the United States during the period 1946-1965 had extended
economic and military assistance to less developed areas in
excess of a hundred billion dollars.

As the Khrushchev era came to an end in the early 'sixties,
the Soviets had succeeded in projecting Soviet power and
influence into the Third World, and did so cheaply. At the
same time, they went about this task, except in the case of
Cuba, in a way that minimized conflict with the militarily
and economically more powerful United States.

Problems of Violence, Credibility & Control

The Cuban missile crisis in 1962 clearly demonstrated to the Soviets that their involvement in Third World affairs was not without substantial risks. Involvement, particularly where strong U.S. interests were involved, could lead the Kremlin into a conflict with America. This, the Soviets went to great lengths to avoid.

Khrushchev set forth the Soviet case on armed conflict in the nuclear age in his commentary on the 1960 Moscow Declaration of eighty-one communist parties. First, he warned, nuclear war would be catastrophic and had to be avoided. Second, local wars were dangerous because they could escalate and lead to nuclear conflict. National liberation wars, where local revolutionaries were fighting local reactionaries, were just conflicts and would be supported by the Soviet Union. The Kremlin hewed to this line and showed great caution in such local conflicts in Laos, the Congo and Vietnam.

Although there is considerable evidence that Moscow egged the Arabs on against the Israelis in 1967 and in 1973, it showed considerable restraint once their Arab clients had lost on the battlefield; at that point, the Soviets were more than ready to secure a diplomatic solution to bring the conflict to an end. Ironically, President John F. Kennedy misread the Kremlin's intention by believing that its support for national liberation movements was evidence of wholesale Soviet endorsement of local wars. It meant precisely the opposite, as the Chinese were quick to point out. After coming to office in 1961, President Kennedy set out to develop the capability to intervene directly against insurgent movements which he held to be communist-inspired or otherwise dangerous. This policy was soon to lead the United States into more than a decade of military involvement in Southeast Asia, parts of Africa and Central America.

Khrushchev's policies of embracing nationalist leaders created another set of problems for the Soviet leadership. Under this policy of breaking with Stalinist orthodoxy about the unreliability of the "national bourgeoisie," the Kremlin worked closely with India's Jawaharlal Nehru, Ghana's Kwame N'Kruma, Egypt's Gamal Abdel Nasser, Indonesia's Sukarno, Guinea's Sekou Touré, Algeria's Ahmed Ben Bella and other Third World leaders. Under Khrushchev, the Soviets instructed local communist parties to cooperate with these nationalist leaders or even merge their party organizations with those of the nationalists to avoid mistrust or antagonism.

Not infrequently, the fruits of this policy have proved bitter to the Soviet leaders. While anti-Western in outlook, the nationalists often had their own vision of the future, tended to reciprocate Soviet opportunism in their dealings with Moscow, and showed no disposition to step aside for "objective laws of history"; not uncommonly, as has been true in Iraq and Egypt, these leaders have treated the local communist parties with great harshness. In Egypt, Nasser's successor, Anwar al-Sadat, ousted the Russians, a fate that also befell Moscow in Somalia after it had invested considerably in the Socialist government of President Mohamed Siad Barre. Even where the Soviets have managed to retain some influence over nationalist leaders, as in Syria and India, they have used the Kremlin as much for their own purposes as the Russians used them for theirs. Indira Gandhi, for example, refused to endorse the Soviet invasion of Afghanistan.

Having realized their mistake of excessive reliance on "bourgeois nationalism" during the fifties and sixties, the Kremlin has set out on a new strategy for the seventies and eighties. In some cases, as with Syria, Algeria, Iraq and India, they have continuted to work with non-communist socialists of one kind or other. In other countries in Asia and Africa, where local communist parties have shown strength, Soviet strategy has been to help them gain state power. Once this has been done, as has happened in Angola, Ethiopia, South Yemen and Afghanistan, Moscow has spared no effort in assisting them to consolidate their hold. Among the methods employed to assure continued communist rule are economic and military aid, diplomatic support at the regional and international levels and, where necessary, the despatch of Cuban, East German and Soviet troops to protect the fledgling regime from hostile forces. Cuban soldiers and Soviet military staff officers were used to help the demoralized Ethiopian army repel invading Somali forces in the Ogaden province.

Having communist governments in power in Third World countries yields important dividends to the Kremlin. Such governments, unlike those led by old-line, anti-Western nationalists, will almost certainly be more responsive to Soviet wishes. Not surprisingly, the puppet government installed by Vietman in Phnom Penh following its invasion of Cambodia, a move that had the blessing of the Soviet Union, was recognized only by communist states that gave unswerving loyalty to Moscow. Thus, Moscow's new communist allies in Asia and Africa joined with Moscow's faithful regimes in Eastern Europe plus Cuba and Mongolia in a critical test of allegiance to the Soviet Union by recognizing the Vietnamese-installed regime in Phnom Penh. The same roster of countries endorsed the Soviet invasion of Afghanistan by recognizing the Soviet-installed government of Kamal Babrak.

Communist control in Third World countries has made them far more amenable to Soviet influence than would have otherwise been possible. Too many things have gone awry, as far as the Soviets are concerned, when Third World countries are ruled by the so-called bourgeois nationalist leaders. In some, military coups have brought less friendly leaders to power, as occurred in Algeria in the early 1960s with the overthrow of Ben Bella; not uncommonly, the Soviets have encountered setbacks when more normal means of succession are at work. Nasser's successor, Anwar

Sadat, became a bitter foe of the Soviets, expelled Soviet advisers from Egypt and renounced the treaty of friendship linking the two countries. Democratic elections in India in 1977 resulted in the political defeat of Mrs. Gandhi, a staunch ally of the Kremlin.

One strategem employed by the Soviets in cementing ties with key Third World countries is the increasingly familiar treaty of friendship. Moscow has symbolized its thrust toward global diplomacy over the past decade by signing ten formal friendship treaties. Although the West may regard them as merely symbols, of little value in themselves, the Soviets take a different view. They see their prestige riding on the documents, which tend to lend authority and legitimacy to their relations abroad. This helps explain the strong Soviet reaction whenever a friendship treaty is canceled by another country, even when relations had been poor for some time beforehand. In the past several years this has happened to three of these documents when Egypt, Somalia and the People's Republic of China formally annulled their treaties. This has left treaties in force between Moscow and India (signed in1971), Iraq (1972), Angola (1976), Mozambique (1977), Ethiopia, Afghanistan and Vietnam (all 1978) and South Yemen (1979).

One possible reason for the Soviet preference for formal treaties is to reduce internal dissent against the leadership's foreign policies. Assuming that certain elements of the Soviet hierarchy are less enchanted with some of the treaties than the top leadership, it is thought that the leaders can justify developing policies by pointing to the treaties as a legal basis. By and large, developing countries place less stock in the treaties than does their partner, and often view them as means of acquiring financial, military or diplomatic support at a given moment. As has already been noted, three countries abrogated their treaties. On March 15, 1976, Egypt annulled the treaty; Somalia, which signed its treaty October 30, 1974, abrogated it three years later; finally, China, whose treaty with Moscow went back to 1950, cancelled it in April 1979 after having given the required one-year notice.

The documents run for fifteen, twenty or (with Vietnam) for twenty-five years. They define the various fields of cooperation and include clauses on military aid (except with India, which wanted to avoid public mention, and with Vietnam which did not need much). Apart from Afghanistan, each pledges consultation if situations arise that threaten either contracting party. Looser language with Afghanistan simply states that the parties shall consult on all major issues affecting them. Legally, this is less a commitment for the Soviets; in practice, it allows them to act as they see fit. Apparently, even at the time Moscow signed the treaty in 1977 it was troubled by guerrilla opposition to the Marxist government of Nur Mohammed Taraki. The most pointed Soviet commitments are to India and Vietnam. In both treaties, the Kremlin agrees not only to consult, but also to take "appropriate effective measures," if either side is attacked or threatened with attack. Although in both cases the language seems aimed at China, the treaty with Vietnam is warmer and closer than the one with India. This reflects Vietnam's status as a fellow socialist country assigned a key role in containing Peking's influence in Southeast Asia.

The countries that Moscow has chosen to ally itself with in the Third World are of great strategic importance to the Soviets. The Arab world, from Morocco to the Persian Gulf, and South Asia have, over the past twenty-five years, represented the highest priority targets for Soviet diplomatic, economic and military effort. As the Soviets have increased their capacity to project military power further away from their borders, their interest in Africa, notably the Horn, has grown as well. India and Vietnam are important because they help contain Chinese influence in South and Southeast Asia; Iraq and Egypt are politically great prizes because of their strategic location in the Arab world; Ethiopia and Southern Yemen have proved irresistible lures to the Soviets because they lie athwart the Red Sea and close to the major oil tanker lanes in the Arabian Sea and the Gulf of Suez. And Afghanistan is important because it is situated on the Soviet Union's southern border and, if under Moscow's control, would provide it with an important platform for projecting military power and political influence in Iran and Pakistan. In the light of these concerns, the Soviets require something more solid than the friendship treaty to protect their interests in these key developing countries. The Soviet military intervention in Afghanistan, a country outside the Warsaw Pact, and one that has been considered part of the non-aligned group of nations, strongly suggests that Moscow will henceforth not be reluctant to invoke the so-called Brezhnev Doctrine in socialist countries even if they are outside the recognized Soviet satellite groups of countries in Eastern Europe.

Brezhnev Doctrine

The original Brezhnev Doctrine, which declared that the sovereignty of communist countries was limited by the overall needs of the Soviet bloc as defined by Moscow, emerged in an article in *Pravda*, the Soviet Communist Party newspaper, in September 1968, five weeks after the Soviet Union and four allies invaded Czechoslovakia. The doctrine was contributed by Western political commentators solely to Leonid I. Brezhnev, then and still the head of the Soviet Communist Party, as a way of holding him responsible for the invasion of Czechoslovakia. The *Pravda* article was actually signed by a propaganda specialist, Sergei Kovalev.

The Soviets may be resorting to the same ideological rationale for justifying their intervention in Afghanistan. Several weeks after the Afghanistan invasion, an article appeared in the Moscow weekly *Novoye Vremya* which offered much the same justification for this action as the *Pravda* article did twelve years earlier. In both articles there are similiarities in themes and argumentation. Both proceed, for instance, from the premise of an international class struggle in which the revolutionary movement must prevail. The *Novoye Vremya* article, which was unsigned, suggesting to some analysts that it had considerable authority, said that "matters are sometimes portrayed as though the United States and the Soviet Union were equally to blame in the situation which has formed around Afghanistan (and in several similar cases in the past in other regions)." It then went on to declare: "This way of putting the question is absolutely false since it totally ignores the main point: the fundamental difference between the nature and goals of the foreign policy of socialism and imperialism."

Foreign analysts called attention to a parallel argument in *Pravda* in 1968, which described criticism of the Czechoslovakia invasion "as based on an abstract non-class approach," and added: "From a Marxist point of view, the norms of law, including the norms of mutual relations of the Socialist countries, cannot be interpreted narrowly, formally and in isolation from the general context of class struggle in the world."

The essence of the Brezhnev Doctrine as defined in the *Pravda* article was: "The sovereignty of each Socialist country cannot be opposed to the interests of the world of Socialism, of the world revolutionary movement." The *Novoye Vremya* statement, in the view of some American government analysts, goes well beyond the original doctrine by creating what one called "a new ideological dimension." These analysts drew attention to a passage that they said extended the justification for armed intervention by the Soviet Union well beyond the confines of the traditional bloc allies to any developing country beset by political unrest. The passage said: "The question arises: What is the international solidarity of revolutionaries? Does it consist only of moral and diplomatic support and verbal wishes for success, or does it also consist, under justified, extraordinary conditions, in rendering material aid, including military aid, all the more so when it is a case of blatant, massive outside intervention? The history of the revolutionary movement confirms the moral and political rightness of this form of aid and support. This was the case, for instance, in Spain in the '30s and in China in the '20s and '30s. Now that the system of Socialist states exists, to deny the right to such aid would simply be strange."

The inference drawn by some American analysts is that any less developed country proclaiming communist goals and open to Soviet assistance could find itself liable to "protective" intervention on the lines of the Soviet move into Afghanistan on December 27, 1979. Veljko Micunovic's intimate account of his experiences as Yugoslavia's ambassdor to the Kremlin from 1956 to 1958 sheds some interesting light on Russian behavior toward their socialist allies in time of crisis.* His recollections of the situation in Hungary in 1956, for instance, are a pointed reminder of Afghanistan in 1979. Micunovic, whose access to life inside the Kremlin was shared by few if any other foreigners during this or any other period of Soviet rule, relates that Khrushchev decided to send troops into Hungary when the situation there began to unravel. The feisty Soviet leader flew secretly to Yugoslavia to tell Tito that he intended to invade because otherwise, "the West would say we are either stupid or weak." According to the ambassador, Khrushchev added that the Soviet army lobby in the Kremlin "was one of the reasons they were intervening in Hungary." Micunovic concludes that slogans like "peaceful co-existence" apply only outside the "socialist camp," that "Russians do not allow that anybody can be a Marxist and not be cut to their pattern," and that "what has emerged instead is a relationship of big and small states under socialism which is not substantially different from the relationship between big and small countries under capitalism."

A central feature of Soviet foreign policy since the late fifties has been the need to avoid conflict with the United

---

*Veljko Micunovic: *Moscow Diary* (Translated by David Floyd), New York, Doubleday & Co.

States. This approach spawned the policy of detente with the West. Such a policy was particularly important during the late fifties, the sixties and the early seventies when the Soviets were still inferior to the U.S. in both conventional and nuclear weapons. In the Third World, the Kremlin, although cautiously supporting wars of national liberation, avoided taking sides in local wars lest this lead to a confrontation with the U.S. Even in areas adjoining the Soviet Union, which the Kremlin adjudged vital to its interests, such as the Middle East and the Persian Gulf, the Soviets limited their involvement in conflict situations. After the Arab defeats in 1967 and 1973, they showed no disposition to provide direct military assistance to Syria and Egypt when Washington signaled its intention that it would not tolerate any such intervention. Actually, the mutual forbearance of the two superpowers in Third World conflicts was not a matter of happenstance. Perhaps the outstanding achievement of the Nixon-Kissinger foreign policy was its recognition that militant competition between Washington and Moscow posed a threat to the security of both, and that it could and should be regulated. In addition to a number of agreements to this effect, the 1972 summit meeting between Nixon and Brezhnev produced a joint "Declaration of Principles" which laid down ground rules in this matter. The declaration stated that "the USA and the USSR have a special responsibility... to do everything in their power so that conflicts or situations will not arise which would serve to increase international tensions.... Both sides recognize that efforts to obtain unilateral advantage at the expense of the other, directly or indirectly, are inconsistent with these objectives." The two countries agreed to consultations between them to deal with such situations.

The agreement began to come apart soon after the Portuguese revolution liberated Portugal's territories in Africa. Both the Soviet Union and the United States, without significant or effective consultation between them, supported a different faction in the Angolan civil war which raged in

1975, accompanying that support with a drumfire of mutual recrimination. Neither Moscow nor Washington seemed to weigh seriously whether what it could hope to gain in Angola was remotely comparable to the damage being inflicted on their mutual relations and hence on their overall security. The United States, still chastened by its overinvolvement and defeat in Vietnam, tended to be cautious about involvement elsewhere in the Third World. Thus, when the Ford Administration wanted to take a firm role when Cuban troops first emerged on the African stage in Angola in 1975, Congress firmly opposed it. Congress adamantly refused to countenance Central Intelligence Agency operations against Dr. Neto's Marxist-Leninist MPLA by providing covert support to his cheif opponent, Jonas Savimbi.

Some critics of this Congressional intrusion in foreign policy matters have claimed that the United States, by not taking up the Soviet challenge in Angola, virtually invited Soviet moves in other troubled Third World countries having strategic importance. Whether this is true or not, the Kremlin, which in the past had been much less adventuresome that the U.S. in the Third World arena, began to exercise its newly acquired capabilities, including Cuban willingness to serve as a military pawn, and to intervene, with little regard for the Declaration of Principles, in a series of critical areas, notably Ethiopia, Yemen and Afghanistan. In addition, the Soviets agreed to sign a new treaty of friendship with the Vietnamese. This treaty triggered a chain-reaction—Vietnamese invasion of Cambodia, Chinese attack on Vietnam—which opened up a new theater of great-power confrontation, this time between the two major communist powers. This conflict, nevertheless, also has affected the United States, both because of its possible threat to Thailand and because of possible hostilities along the Sino-Soviet border.

Thus, within eight years after the signing of the Declaration of Principles, designed to limit super-power competition in the Third World, that competition has once again risen to cold war proportions. The United States, through the Carter Doctrine, has served notice on the Soviet Union that it would repel by all means necessary an attack on the Persian Gulf. It has sought to give credibility to this pledge by strengthening its fleet in the Indian Ocean, raising military expenditures, acquiring new bases in the Persian Gulf region and Horn of Africa and reducing trade and embargoing the sale of wheat to the Soviet Union. The latter, showing no signs of backing down, has been consolidating its position in Afghanistan and making broad gestures of friendship to the Iranian revolutionary leadership. "As the 1980s begin," wrote Richard J. Barnet, the American scholar, who has written extensively on U.S.-Soviet relations, "the world seems closer to a major war than at any time since the 1930s. Detente has broken down under the pressure of a new militarist foreign policy consensus in the U.S., and the Soviet invasion of Afghanistan. A political chain reaction is building to the point where the fragile bonds that inhibit escalation to wider war may be snapped."*

Causes of Growing Superpower Hostility

The factors leading to the deterioration of U.S.-Soviet relations are numerous and complex. In substantial measure, they can be traced to bilateral differences over the very nature of the relationship between the superpowers. Beyond that, there have been important differences over specific issues, notably human rights, disarmament, China and the Arab-Israel conflict. The bad relations are also the product of bold Soviet initiatives in critically important Third World countries, particularly Ethiopia, Southern Yemen and Afghanistan. It may be argued that Soviet activity in the Horn of Africa and Red Sea areas were a response to U.S. efforts to exclude the Soviets from the Middle East attempts at a

---

*"Old Rules are off with Superpowers Fencing again," *Newsday*, January 15, 1980.

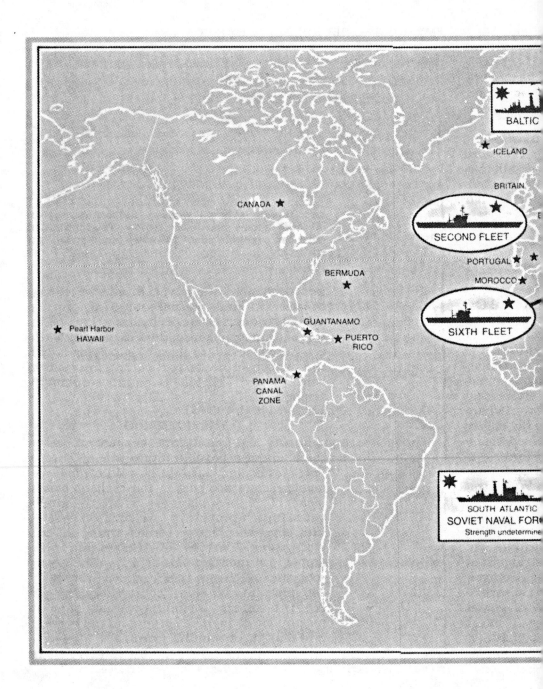

BALTIC

★ ICELAND

BRITAIN

SECOND FLEET

PORTUGAL ★

MOROCCO ★

SIXTH FLEET

★ CANADA

BERMUDA ★

★ Pearl Harbor
HAWAII

GUANTANAMO ★

★ PUERTO
RICO

PANAMA
CANAL
ZONE

SOUTH ATLANTIC
SOVIET NAVAL FORC
Strength undetermine

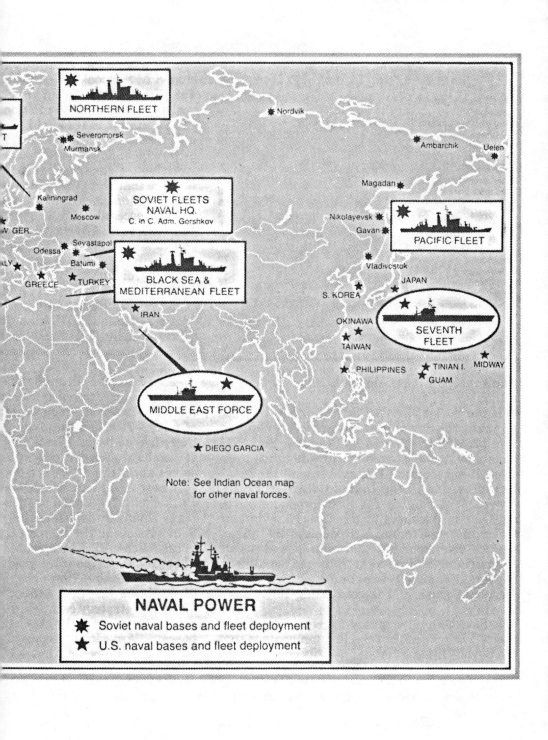

NORTHERN FLEET

Nordvik

Severomorsk
Murmansk

Ambarchik

Uelen

Kaliningrad

Magadan

SOVIET FLEETS
NAVAL HQ.
C. in C. Adm. Gorshkov

Nikolayevsk

PACIFIC FLEET

Moscow

Gavan

W GER

Odessa

Sevastopol

Vladivostok

Batumi

JAPAN

GREECE   TURKEY

BLACK SEA &
MEDITERRANEAN FLEET

S. KOREA

LY

SEVENTH
FLEET

IRAN

OKINAWA

TAIWAN

MIDWAY

PHILIPPINES

TINIAN I.
GUAM

MIDDLE EAST FORCE

★ DIEGO GARCIA

Note: See Indian Ocean map
for other naval forces.

NAVAL POWER

Soviet naval bases and fleet deployment

U.S. naval bases and fleet deployment

settlement. In October 1977, Washington and Moscow agreed to seek a comprehensive settlement of the conflict by reconvening the Geneva conference under their joint chairmanship. After President Sadat's bold initiative of seeking direct negotiations with Israel, effectively ending Soviet hopes for a Geneva conference, President Carter went along with Cairo. The Soviets, it could be argued, sought to compensate for this rebuff to its interests in a strategic area close to its borders. According to this thesis, the Soviets seized opportunites in the Ethiopian-Somali war, in tensions between North and South Yemen and in Afghanistan.

Perhaps more fundamental in explaining the discord between the United States and the Soviet Union over the past five years is the attitude that the Carter Administration assumed toward its arch rival. The basic relationship between the superpowers became an issue right after President Carter took office in 1977. He and his advisers entered office dedicated to reversing many of the basic foreign policy themes of the Nixon-Ford-Kissinger era. During this era, U.S. policy was to treat the Soviet Union as the most important other country in the world. Relations with the Soviet Union were considered "central to the development of detente." Moscow was never left in any doubt that Washington valued detente, wanted to keep it going, and therefore wanted to cultivate the best possible relations.

President Carter's national security adviser, Zbigniew Brzezinski, maintained that under Nixon and Ford, Secretary of State Henry A. Kissinger had placed too great an emphasis on dealing with Moscow, and he promised that the new administration would spend more time shoring up relations with Western Europe, Japan and China. A specialist in Soviet affairs known for his hard-line views, Mr. Brzezinski held that the previous administration had spent too much time fostering detente with Moscow. By downgrading the importance of the Soviet Union, he maintained, Washington would have more time to cultivate relations with China and other emerging nations in Asia, Latin America and Africa.

The Carter State Department under Secretary Cryus R. Vance, which was often at loggerheads with Brzezinski over important issues, reenforced this trend of downgrading ties with the Kremlin. Vance was assisted by a group of young foreign affairs specialists dedicated to finding solutions to conflicts in southern Africa and other turbulent regions and carrying out a "new agenda" with such goals as restraining exports of conventional arms. This policy emphasized Washington's relations with Third World countries rather than containment of Soviet expansionism. Ironically, as relations with Moscow deteriorated in the wake of the Soviet invasion of Afghanistan, it was scarely possible to play down these ties. The threatening situation in the Persian Gulf, exacerbated by the Soviet military intervention in Afghanistan, generated tensions that could be dealt with only at the highest levels. As one White House aide observed barely a fortnight after the Kremlin's move into Afghanistan, "But ironically for Zbig [Brzezinski], relations with Moscow have become so bad that everybody recognizes that the Soviet Union has once again become the top priority in American policy."

There have been other aspects of President Carter's policies in foreign affairs that contributed to the growing falling out with Moscow. His strong emphasis on "human rights" was deeply resented; although not above intervening in the internal affairs of other countries, the Soviets took exception to this U.S. policy on the ground that it constituted interference in the internal affairs of their country. The failure of disarmament talks to make much headway has also weakened detente. Significantly, President Carter came to office pledged to dampen East-West military competition. The Administration's handling of the disarmament question was not to the liking of the Soviets. Early on in his Administration, President Carter proposed a major reduction in strategic missiles which fell far short of the number that had been agreed to by President Ford and Soviet Communist Party leader Leonid Brezhnev at the Vladivostok summit in 1974. The Soviets were caught off guard and embarrassed by the American initiative, which they felt was a propaganda ploy. The Soviets were also unhappy over the lack of progress being made in the U.S. Senate in regard to the ratification of the SALT II agreement, which was signed in Vienna in June 1979. Their displeasure was in evidence before President Carter requested that the Senate shelve the treaty following the Soviet intervention in Afghanistan. Perhaps of even greater concern to Moscow was Washington's decision to urge its NATO allies to install a new generation of medium-range missiles. The Soviets had unsuccessfully sought to forestall this move by announcing a unilateral withdrawal of a limited number of its troops stationed in East Germany. This gesture did little to soften the growing apprehension in Western capitals over the large increase in Soviet tanks deployments in the plains of central Europe.

Relations between United States and China have also been a source of growing Soviet apprehension. Efforts between Peking and Moscow to resolve basic differences broke down in late 1979. As Sino-Soviet ties deteriorated, relations between the United States and Peking improved. This was evidenced by the Carter Administration's grant of most-favored-nation trading status to the Chinese without according the same benefit to the Soviets. As normal trading ties between the United States and the People's Republic of China have blossomed, there has been growing signs that Washington would be willing to sell sophisticated technology to the Chinese to help modernize their backward economy. More ominous to the Soviets have been the growing signs of U.S. willingness to sell sophisticated armaments to Peking. According to a report by *The Daily Mail*, a British mass-circulation daily, Brezhnev had issued a grim though indirect warning to the United States toward the end of January 1980 against arming China with nuclear weapons. Repeatedly, the Soviets had warned the United States against playing the "China card." The Soviets, too, had unsuccessfully sought to play this card. Just before the

Vienna summit to sign the SALT II treaty, Moscow had
agreed to talks with Peking on normalizing government-to-
government relations. These talks came a cropper. Actually,
relations between these two communist powers had fallen to
new lows, particularly because the Chinese feared the
Soviets were attempting to encircle them by building up
Vietnam; the Chinese were of the view that the Vietnamese
attack on Cambodia had been encouraged by the Kremlin.

Soviet policies in Third World countries were another,
and potent, factor disturbing ties with the United States.
The Kremlin had pursued a vigorous policy in important
Third World countries, promoting its own interests and
opposing those of the United States and the West. This was
evident in Ethiopia, Southern Yemen and Afghanistan.
There had been strong suspicions in Western capitals that
the Soviets were behind the unrest in mineral-rich Shaba,
the southern province of Zaire, and attempted coups in the
Sudan and Somalia. The United States was also deeply
disturbed over Soviet support for the government of Libyan
strongman Muammar al-Qaddafi. Thus, while the Kremlin
had long sought military detente with the United States
symbolized by the SALT II treaty—it has pursued an activist policy in strategic Third World countries. The Soviets
have insisted they have an unqualified right to support
"national liberation struggles" which in their eyes are "just"
struggles. They have, as a result, resisted efforts by the
Carter Administration to link progress on SALT or other
bilateral issues with their activities in Third World countries. Until the Soviet invasion of Afghanistan, the Carter
Administration reluctantly went along with this approach.
Secretary of State Cyrus Vance held that if progress on
SALT II were conditioned on Soviet restraint in regional
conflicts, there could be no progress on the other vital issues
affecting the superpowers. The secretary was of the view that
individual problems with the Soviets could be worked out
on a case-by-case basis. National security adviser Brzezinski, by contrast, had tended to view Soviet actions in the

Third World within a broader geo-strategic framework. It was he who first called attention to the so-called "arc of crisis." Underlying his view was a belief that Soviet actions in the Third World were not isolated events but part of a strategic plan for dominance.

From the very beginning of the Carter Administration, differences over the Vance and Brzezinski approaches in viewing Soviet Third World policies had plagued the handling of foreign policy. The departure of Vance from the Administration in March 1980, over the use of force in the abortive attempt to rescue the American hostages in Teheran, was an unambiguous signal that the Brzezinski approach would be in the ascendancy. Even before the Secretary of State's resignation, there were clear indications that this tougher line had been accepted by President Carter. The so-called "Carter Doctrine" was to put the Soviets on notice that their invasion of Afghanistan was a threat not only to the independence of that non-aligned Muslim country, but also a threat to the Persian Gulf and Southwest Asia.

Washington Turns to Pakistan

Following the Soviet invasion in Afghanistan, the Carter Administration made a strong effort to improve ties with its erstwhile ally, Pakistan. The government in Islamabad responded positively but in a cautious manner to these advances.

That the military government in Pakistan felt threatened by the Soviet presence in neighboring Afghanistan could not be doubted. Relations had never been too cordial between these two Islamic countries. Kabul had long supported claims for independence by some groups in Pakistan's Pushtu province. There was also now the real possibility that the Soviet-controlled government in Kabul would supply material support for the restive Baluchi populations, which had been seeking political autonomy. Pakistan, moreover, was feeling directly the effects of the growing rebellion against the Soviet takeover. Scores of thousands of refugees were fleeing to Pakistan to escape the fighting. This placed a heavy financial burden on the already hard-pressed Pakistan treasury. There was also the fear that Soviet troops might cross over into Pakistan in pursuit of Afghan resistance fighters.

A more basic threat was that the Soviet Union now stood astride the Khyber Pass. Afghanistan, which historically had served as a buffer state between Russia and the Indian subcontinent, could now be expected to serve as a tool of Soviet diplomacy. It had surrendered its status as a nonaligned country for the role of a Soviet satellite.

The Russian invasion of Afghanistan served to place Pakistan in the international limelight. The martial law government of General Zia ul-Huq, which had been shunned by the U.S., was now being courted by the Carter Administration. This opened possibilities allowing Islamabad to break out of its isolation and to shore up its position at home. Thus, the Soviet invasion of Afghanistan, which, although not without risks of a potentially grave nature to Pakistan, afforded new and unexpected benefits for General Zia and his government. Foremost among these were Washington's efforts to promote a political reconciliation with him. Tied to this new development were offers of military and economic aid. Such aid was essential for the government, whose foreign credit had been virtually exhausted and whose military establishment was woefully run down.

Washington's Concern over Pakistan

The Carter Administration's main concern in Southwest Asia was the very real possibility of a Soviet move that could undermine Pakistan. The United States feared that Pakistan, which was economically and militarily vulnerable, and had not fully recovered from the loss of its eastern wing in 1971 as a result of a disastrous war with India, would not be able to withstand the pressures generated by the invasion of Afghanistan. Political instability in Pakistan could tempt the Kremlin to pursue its long-nourished dream of securing a warm-water port in the Arabian Sea. The key to this would be the politically volatile area of Baluchistan, whose disaffected population might be encouraged to break away from the repressive government in Islamabad and form an independent Baluchistan. The creation of such a state under Moscow's tutelage would give enhanced political leverage over the entrance to the Persian Gulf and allow for an increased Soviet naval presence in the Indian Ocean.

A strengthened Pakistan, the leaders in Washington held, might deter the Kremlin from pushing its gains in Afghanistan too far. A Soviet move across the Khyber Pass, an unlikely but not impossible step, would have serious military and political implications for the entire region. China, which was drawing closer to the U.S. in the wake of the Soviet Afghan move, also had reason to be concerned by such a possible Soviet thrust. The Chinese tacitly endorsed Washington's efforts to rearm Pakistan, with which they had a close relationship. A strong and friendly Pakistan could serve as a possible base for funneling military supplies to the Afghan tribesmen fighting the Soviets. Although the United States had not committed itself to such a course of action, it would not be unreasonable to assume that such a clandestine policy would be pursued. A number of Senators, including Senator Patrick Moynihan of New York, had called for an easing of restraints on the CIA as one way of promoting American interests in this vital area. A strong Pakistan, in addition, could serve as a counterweight to India, which is linked to the Soviet Union by a treaty of friendship. The return of Indira Gandhi as Prime Minister of India in January 1980 raised concerns in Pakistan and China that she would bring back her first administration's policies of strengthening ties with Moscow. Delhi's initial reaction of not condemning the Soviet invasion of Afghanistan appeared to bear out fears that Mrs. Gandhi was bent on revitalizing the Moscow connection.

It was against this background that President Carter sent national security adviser Brzezinski to Pakistan in February to develop a new basis of friendship with the martial law government of General Zia. It was not known what came

out of this meeting with Zia. Nonetheless, it appeared that
initial American action to win over the Zia regime had not
been very successful. Despite Pakistan's hard-pressed financial situation, Zia turned down Washington's offer of four
hundred million dollars worth of military and economic aid.
The general brusquely dismissed the offer as "peanuts." For
this sum, he let it be known, it was not in Pakistan's interest
to antagonize the Soviets by drawing close to its one-time
patron. Such an amount, he stated, could not begin to buy
for Pakistan the kind of military equipment his generals
needed.

Although Zia rejected the offer, it did not appear at this
early stage that he was ruling out the possibility of close ties
later. There was evidence that he might be trying for better
terms. Whatever the motives, initial attempts to effect a
reconciliation with Pakistan did not get far. For its part, the
Carter Administration allowed the matter to stand there,
not wishing to offer any more—at least for the while. Actually, this was not the response it had expected from
Pakistan.

These initial unsuccessful attempts of reconciliation can
be better understood against the background of past U.S.-
Pakistani relations.

Past U.S.-Pakistani Relations

During the 'fifties and early 'sixties, ties between the two
countries had prospered. During these years, Pakistan
received vast sums of U.S. economic and military assistance.
It was also closely linked to the United States through the
CENTO and SEATO military pacts. Perhaps of even
greater importance was that it was tied to the United States
through an executive agreement that President Dwight D.
Eisenhower had negotiated in 1959. The agreement pledged
Washington's support in the event Pakistan became the
victim of a communist-inspired military invasion. So close
was the relationship between Washington and Islamabad

that many educated Pakistanis half-jokingly referred to their country as the "fifty-first state."

As a consequence of this special relationship, Pakistan became the linch-pin of American foreign policy in Southwest Asia and on the Indian subcontinent. An immediate cost of this, which was not fully appreciated at the time, was to alienate India, which drew close to the Soviet Union. For the latter, this tie to Delhi strengthened its position on the subcontinent. By strengthening India, which, since the 1962 war with China had been on bad terms with Peking, the Soviets opened a new front against China along its borders with India.

After an extended period of friendship, relations between Pakistan and the United States began to cool, largely as a result of Pakistan's wars with India, which turned out to be military disasters. Many educated Pakistanis shared the view that Washington had reneged on its commitments by not backing their country in the 1965 conflict. And despite President Nixon's much publicized "tilt" toward Pakistan during the 1971 war, the feeling had taken hold that he did not do nearly enough to help the government to put down the Bengali rebellion in the eastern wing of the country. With massive assistance from the Indian army, this breakaway province went on to establish the independent state of Bangladesh. Pakistan also felt that the United States had not recognized or rewarded it for the role it had played in bringing together Washington and Peking. It was generally known that when President Nixon made his historic trip to Peking, the Pakistanis, who enjoyed close ties with China, helped facilitate the initial contacts.

Islamabad's complaints about the weakened U.S. support were not without additional justification. The U.S. withdrawal from Vietnam and from Southeast Asia had resulted in a diminished overall commitment to the defense of Asia against communism. The United States had ceased to view China as a threat to Asia. This change in perception removed an important reason for maintaining a forward military position in southwest Asia. Washington, in recognition of India's preeminent position on the subcontinent, was now becoming committed to striking a more balanced policy between Delhi and Islamabad.

As a result of these developments, the United States and Pakistan gradually drew apart. This trend received added impetus in 1977 following the military coup that brought General Zia ul-Huq to power. Early promises by the military rulers to hold elections within ninety days were not kept, and the country passed into the grip of yet another military dictatorship. The 1977 coup, and the political repression that followed, deeply troubled the Carter Administration. An important aspect of President Carter's foreign policy was maintaining human rights abroad. As the military extended its rule, holding out little promise of a return to civilian government, the Carter Administration had even less reason to work closely with the authorities in Islamabad.

Yet another shock to relations between the two countries came with the execution of former President Zulfikar Ali Bhutto. Bhutto, one of Pakistan's few rulers who came to power by the route of democratic elections, was imprisoned by Zia following his overthrow. The deposed president was subsequently convicted of charges of complicity in a murder scheme involving a political rival. Depsite appeals from the leaders of many countries, General Zia was not inclined to spare Bhutto's life. The former president, whose own rule was tarnished by the repressive policies he had pursued in Baluchistan, died on the gallows. Zia's refusal to exercise clemency led many Pakistanis to conclude that as long as Bhutto remained alive, he posed a threat to the shaky regime of the generals in Islamabad.

Ties between the United States and Pakistan reached an all-time low in November 1979 with the sacking of the American embassy in Islamabad by an Islamic mob. What provoked the incident, in which two Americans lost their lives and the embassy was burned to the ground, was a false report from Teheran that the United States was involved in an attack on the Grand Mosque in Mecca. The slow response of Pakistan's martial law authorities in dispersing the mob served to strain relations with Washington. Many observers asserted that this delayed defence of the Americans was prompted by Zia's realization of the explosive potential of any official response to the mob action and the threat that this would pose to his own increasingly troubled rule.

The president's concern, in the face of clearly profound Islamic feeling among his own people, was reflected in his support for Iran and its militant Muslim leaders. Their fundamentalist fervor appears to have tapped a deep lode of political and religious support in other Muslim countries. Zia had expressed concern over the possible use by the United States of force in freeing the hostages. At the same time that he was grappling with the Islamic tide unleashed by Iran's Ayatollah Ruhollah Khomeini both within and beyond Iran's borders, Zia had been attempting to improve relations with Washington. This effort could be seriously hampered by the distinct anti-Western tinge infusing the fervor of his Muslim countrymen. Many diplomats held that Zia had to think long and hard before sending the troops against the mob, which started with students but then swelled with the addition of toughs. "Zia had troubles," said one non-Western diplomat in Islamabad. "He had to walk a thin line between keeping order and not angering the students." Overall, the incident revealed how little room the regime had for political maneuver in questions relating to political issues affected by Islamic fervor.

The Soviet invasion of Afghanistan made both countries aware of the necessity of putting aside past differences and establishing a firm basis of political cooperation. The Soviet presence near the historic Khyber Pass made it more important than ever, according to the prevailing political viewpoint in Washington, to strengthen Pakistan. U.S. intelligence analysts have pointed to Pakistan's geographical position as a potential advantage to the West. Rearmed and

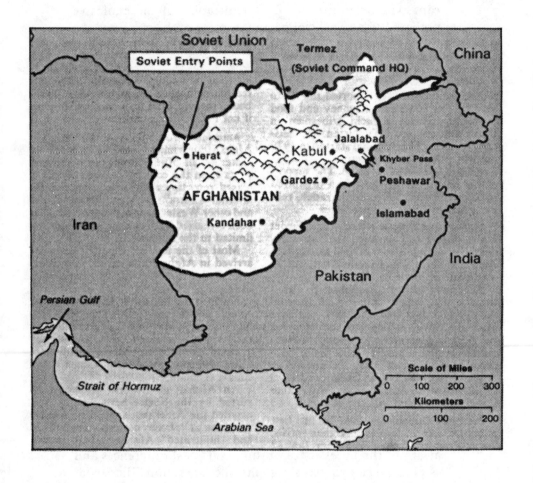

modernized, Pakistani forces could balance a Soviet military presence in Afghanistan to some extent, or, should the Russian troops be withdrawn, balance the Afghan forces stiffened by Soviet advisers and technicians who would remain. Should the Afghan insurgency prosper, which was far from certain in the immediate aftermath of the Soviet invasion, the 1,200-mile-long porous, mountainous frontier would provide routes for moving arms to the rebels. Some sources questioned whether the Pakistani government would approve such arms transfers or even continue to act as a sanctuary for rebels driven out of their territory. Pakistanis have readily conceded that their country, should it become the source of increased aid to the rebels, would be open to Soviet reprisals. Not a few American planners take a similar view. They also recognize that an American program to rearm Pakistan might expose it to serious pressure from India—generally acknowledged to be Asia's biggest military power after China.

As for President Zia, a rapprochement with the U.S. could yield considerable benefits for his county and shore up his own regime. In January 1980, he stated succinctly that what Pakistan wants is "a good treaty of friendship and, in conjunction with others, economic and military assistance." Although he ruled out the possibility of an American base or a substantial American military presence in his country, Zia did say he wished to strengthen defensive ties with Washington. Specifically, he stated that the 1959 executive agreement linking Pakistan and the United States should be replaced by a formal treaty. He also insisted that Pakistan should be allowed to acquire a wide range of such weapons as anti-tank guns. In stressing their defensive nature, he said: "Pakistan does not want any weapons which could create a scare in our neighbors, particularly India."

Aiding Pakistan: A Political Quandry

The Carter Administration's four-hundred-million-dollar aid package could hardly be considered a major initiative in

winning Pakistan over to America's emerging containment
policy in Southwest Asia in the post-Afgan period. Actually
the money was to be used for two purposes: two hundred
million dollars was to go for economic assistance, and the
balance was to be used for the purchase of military equipment. In rejecting the aid offer as "peanuts," General Zia
warned that "Pakistan will not buy its security with four
hundred million dollars." Actually, the relatively small sum
offered to Pakistan appeared to reflect the uncertainties
within the Carter Administration over the establishment of
close ties with the Pakistan of General Zia. Three important
factors were responsible for the Administration's equivocal
attitude. These were: (a) Pakistan's effort to become a
nuclear power; (b) fear of antagonizing India; and (c) the
repressive nature of the Zia regime and its uncertain political
future.

(A) Pakistan's Quest to Go Nuclear

In April 1979, the Carter Administration cut off all aid to
Pakistan after it became convinced that Islamabad was
developing nuclear weapons. The cutoff in assistance,
approximately $40 million in development funds, was man-
dated under the so-called Symington Amendment to the
Foreign Assistance Act, which bars aid to a country that
seems to be developing nuclear weapons. Pakistan was the
first country against which the rule was invoked. This action
was in line with Washington's long-standing policy of dis-
couraging nuclear proliferation.

According to journalistic accounts, President Bhutto had
embarked on a nuclear weapons program after India's successful nuclear test explosion in May 1974. CBS television
news reported June 11 and 12, 1979 that Pakistan, with
financial help from Colonel Muammar al-Qaddafi, the
Libyan leader, was building an "Islamic bomb" to threaten
Israel, Egypt or others. The CBS news report traced through
Britain, the Netherlands, West Germany and Switzerland a

"Pakistani shopping trip" to purchase components of a gas centrifuge. This could be used to refine fuel for peaceful power reactors, which Pakistan says is its intent. But, U.S. analysts point out, it could also be used to produce enriched weapons-grade uranium, used in the original U.S. nuclear bomb dropped on Hiroshima in 1945. Pakistan has all along contended that its nuclear program is for peaceful purposes. Pakistan, according to its oft-stated position, has renounced the acquisition of nuclear weapons and stands ready "to sign an agreement with other neighboring countries banning nuclear weapons from south Asia."

American analysts have not contested this. They also agree that Pakistan has been willing to submit to international safeguards on a French-supplied reprocessing plant, if they were to obtain it, and that the Karachi nuclear power plant, built with Canadian technology, is so safeguarded. However, they add, a uranium reprocessing laboratory at a secret location in Pakistan is not subject to International Atomic Energy Agency or other safeguards.

In light of these findings, the U.S. Administration announced in April 1979 a complete cutoff in aid to Pakistan. In addition, the United States, as Pakistan's chief creditor, has taken a tough stand on the country's appeals for debt rescheduling even though it had just about depleted its foreign exchange reserves. These actions placed a considerable strain on relations between the two countries. Pakistani leaders, who adopted a relatively mild attitude on the matter, expressed surprise that Washington would shape regional ,policies solely in terms of the nuclear issue. The Pakistani view was that at a time when Iran was chaotic and febrile, when the prospects of Soviet intervention in Afghanistan were increasing and when instability threatens much of the region, the United States was foolish to shun Islamabad, which had always regarded itself as one of Washington's most loyal allies.

Depsite this turn in American policy, Pakistani leaders reacted somewhat mildly; there was no outrage, anger or obvious sense of betrayal. Many diplomats believed that this tempered reaction reflected Pakistan's limited ability for political maneuver. One Western diplomat pointedly observed: "Where else can they go?" In terms of power and influence, he said, Pakistan's close ties with China and some wealthy Arab nations cannot supplant the relationship with the United States. Because of the Soviet involvement in Afghanistan, and with Pakistan's commitment to Islamic cultural developments, relations with Moscow were at a low ebb, with little prospect of improvement. However much Pakistan was unhappy with Washington's decision, it could not afford to vent its anger at the United States, thereby having both superpowers as its enemy at the same time.

The urgency of Washington's relations with Pakistan resulting from the Soviet move into Afghanistan prompted the Carter Administration to have second thoughts about using the nuclear issue to determine regional cooperation in Southwest Asia. It extended the offer of $400 million in assistance and, at the same time, a State Department spokesman announced that the United States "reaffirmed" the 1959 executive agreement "in strong terms, assuring Pakistan of the seriousness with which we take our obligations under it." This affirmation of the 1959 agreement was apparently made in response to President Zia's request for a formal treaty between the two countries. There was little disposition, however, to favor treaty relations within the Administration. Instead, the Administration announced "reaffirmation" of the executive agreement. In submitting the aid request, the Administration announced that it would seek a Congressional approval of a waiver of the current law that bars assistance to countries suspected of trying to develop nuclear weapons. Little came of the initiative following Zia's rejection of the proffered financial aid.

General Zia's action came as a disappointment to the Carter Administration, particularly since it announced that Pakistan was the place where it was going to "draw the line" against further Soviet adventures in the Persian Gulf region. Islamabad's decision prompted criticism in the United

States over this aspect of the Administration containment doctrine. It was felt in some quarters that Washington was much too hasty in its approach to Pakistan and that it had not considered all the implications of a policy of *rapprochement* with Pakistan.

The Administration's policy of offering aid to Pakistan without reciprocal concessions regarding its nuclear weapons program raised serious questions about Washington's non-proliferation policies. Such an approach, it was argued, would cause the Administration to lose its scant remaining leverage on Pakistan's nuclear bomb program. Such haste in aiding this country against an extended background of quarreling over the nuclear issue suggested that the Administration had not considered carefully all the ramifications of *rapprochement* with a country where only a few months earlier its embassy had been burned to the ground. Critics argued that the United States should not sacrifice its longer term commitment to curb nuclear proliferation on the subcontinent for short-term benefits of dubious value. A nuclear armed Pakistan could set off a nuclear arms race on the subcontinent with disastrous consequences for both Pakistan and India.

Should Pakistan succeed in developing the bomb, this would almost certainly prompt India to reexamine its nuclear weapons policy. In August 1979, the Indian caretaker Prime Minister, Charan Singh, announced: "If Pakistan sticks to its plans to assemble a bomb, we will have to reconsider the whole question." Until then, India's policy was to maintain a moratorium on nuclear testing; Prime Minister Morarji R. Desai, Indira Gandhi's successor, let it be understood that he accepted General Zia's denials of plans for weapons development. With mounting evidence that Pakistan was bent on developing the bomb, American experts held that India was likely to favor a renewal of emphasis on nuclear weapons.

India has long insisted that it has no desire to build a nuclear weapons stockpile, but it has refused to sign the 1969 treaty to prevent the spread of nuclear weapons, on the ground that the treaty discriminates against nonnuclear nations. Although the U.S. Administration has accepted Delhi's position on the treaty, it had announced that continued American supplies of nuclear fuel would be jeopardized by a refusal to accept international safeguards by March 1980.

Acquisition of the bomb by Pakistan could also have a spill-over effect in the Middle East. Libya, which reportedly has financed Pakistan's nuclear program, could be in line to receive several of the bombs in exchange for its support; it could then proceed to threaten Israel. The Libyan dictator, whose erratic policies at home and abroad have made him something of the odd man out in the Arab world, has been embroiled in conflict with a number of countries, including Egypt, Tunisia, Chad and Uganda. In the event Libya were to acquire atomic bombs, other countries in the region would undoubtedly feel constrained to do the same. It is widely assumed that Israel has a nuclear weapons capability and a small stock of bombs. Iraq, which is trying hard to take on a leading role in Arab politics, has embarked on a nuclear energy program which could be diverted to the production of nuclear weapons. Given the upheaval in the Muslim world and the volatility of Middle East politics, Pakistan's nuclear weapons program could well become a factor in threatening peace and stability in the Middle East.

(B) Upsetting the Political Balance on the Subcontinent

An American policy to rearm Pakistan, regardless of the stated purpose, was bound to provoke deep suspicion in India. Given the history of war between the two countries, any other reaction would almost be unnatural. Delhi has been particularly sensitive to Pakistan's political ties with the United States. In the past, this association, notably through the CENTO and SEATO pacts, and the 1959 executive agreement, had yielded a rich harvest of military aid. Although the assistance was rationalized in terms of containing communist expansionism in the Middle East and Southwest Asia, the weapons ultimately wound up on the battlefields along the Indo-Pakistan border. Thus, India had good reason to suspect a renewal of old ties with the United States.

One major consequence of Washington's close ties with Pakistan in the past was the effect it had on the role of the superpowers on the subcontinent. This relationship served to draw India and the Soviet Union close together, a move formalized by India's signing of a treaty of friendship with Mosocw in 1971. In turn, this chilled U.S.-Indian relations even further. The worsening of relations with Washington, which reached a low point during the 1971 war with Pakistan, had the effect of strengthening Indian resolve to go nuclear. At the time, President Nixon, as part of his celebrated "tilt" toward Pakistan, dispatched the aircraft carrier *Enterprise* toward Indian coastal waters as a gesture of support for the militarily beleaguered Pakistan. This action, it appears, strengthened the argument of the nuclear lobby in Delhi that nuclear weapons would enable the country to deter such "super intervention" in the future.

After President Carter took office, he set out to improve relations with India. The changed political situation on the subcontinent facilitated this initiative. By now, India had become the acknowledged leading power on the subcontinent, and it was somewhat less nervous about the intentions of its rival. The loss by Pakistan of its eastern wing had reduced its role as a regional power and its influence in Washington. Building up Pakistan as a counterweight to India no longer made political sense. The military coup in Pakistan in 1977, which was followed by wide-scale political repression, offended the Carter Administration, which was committed to safeguarding human rights. In the same year, democracy was restored in India as a result of Prime Minister Indira Gandhi's defeat at the polls. Two years earlier, she had declared a national emergency, suspended constitutional guarantees, muzzled the country's free press and locked up thousands of political opponents. Her successor, Morarji Desai, dismantled the system of repression and set the country back again on the course of democracy. Politically, he was somewhat pro-Western in outlook and less inclined toward the Soviet Union. Shortly after he took office, Desai pledged to follow what he called "proper non-alignment," emphasizing that the days of a special role for the Russians in India were over.

As part of this warming trend in U.S.-Indian relations, President Carter paid a brief visit to India in 1978. The President also said he looked with sympathy on India's longstanding request for nuclear fuel for a power plant near Bombay. After the 1974 Indian atomic explosion, the United States had halted the shipment of enriched uranium for that plant, thereby creating an important irritant in relations between the two countries. The Carter Administration's decision in early 1977 to veto a proposed sale of American A-7 fighter-bombers to Pakistan also went down well in India, as did his decision to terminate economic aid. These actions were intended to reduce New Delhi's incentives to acquire nuclear weapons. Ironically, Carter's "tilt" toward India may have served only to intensify Pakistan's atomic ambitions.

The Soviet invasion of Afghanistan led to a quick, and one might say major, change toward Pakistan. After having cut off aid, the Administration was now prepared to extend both economic and military assistance to General Zia's regime. It reaffirmed the 1959 executive agreement with a country that Washington believed was on the way to making its own nuclear weapons and was known for abuses of human and political rights. For an Administration committed to expanding human rights around the world and to halting the spread of nuclear weapons, this was a policy change of large proportions. In a statement before a Senate committee in February 1980, Secretary of State Cyrus Vance summarized the Administration's position on these matters: "This does not signal a lessening of our commitment to nuclear nonproliferation.... It does signal our determination to help a country that faces the threat of Soviet combat forces and combat operations on its border." Conceding human rights abuses by the Zia government, abuses that a State Department report was to lay out starkly soon after, Vance went on to state: "There are times when one, because of security interests, has to accept, for the moment anyway, human rights situations which we deplore." Significantly, there was considerable political support for the Carter policy toward Pakistan in Congress, which showed signs of approving the necessary legislation to put it into effect. General Zia's decision not to accept the proffered four-hundred-million-dollar aid package halted, at least for the while, the Administration's attempts at reconciliation with him.

The situation with India in the post-Afghan period was more complicated. Mrs. Gandhi was not a popular figure on Capitol Hill. She did not help improve her popularity by her initial equivocal remarks on the Soviet move into Afghanistan. There remained strong suspicions regarding her nuclear weapons policies. These had been strengthened by India's refusal to become a signatory to the non-proliferation act. Despite this, the Carter Administration, in early 1980, went ahead with moves to improve relations with Delhi by agreeing to send two shipments of enriched uranium that was provided for under a 1963 agreement with India. The Administration took this position to keep on good terms with the Gandhi government. Not to do so, it argued, could prompt India to abrogate the 1963 accord and pursue an even more independent nuclear policy.

Deputy Secretary of State Warren M. Christopher, in a statement to the Senate Foreign Relations and Government Affairs Committees in mid-June 1980 further stated: "Mrs. Gandhi's government has taken positions on several important matters, which we welcome, and has signaled to us that it wants a constructive relationship." In particular, he said, Delhi had "moved from an uncritical view of recent events in

Afghanistan to one opposing the Soviet invasion and calling
for prompt Soviet withdrawal." In urging Congress not to
veto the shipment of the nuclear fuel, which it could do
under the 1978 Nuclear Nonproliferation Act, Christopher
asserted that India had come to view the fuel issue as "an
index of U.S. interest in maintaining good relations." Many
members of Congress did not go along with this reasoning,
and the Senate barely defeated a move to block the shipment
of the fuel.

(C) The Repressive Nature of the Zia Regime

In considering whether to form an alliance with Pakistan
to hold back the threat coming from Afghanistan, the United
States has had to determine the health of the body politic of
this military-ruled country. If the revolution in Iran has any
meaning for the West, some American circles assert, it is that
alliances with dictators cannot over the long run hope to
succeed; such strongmen lack popular support and are
vulnerable to the wrath of the suppressed population regardless how much military power they appear to command. All
the modern weapons at the shah's disposal proved of little
value in maintaining him in power once the revolution in
Iran gained momentum. In Pakistan, there remained a
serious question as to how stable the government was and
how much support it commanded among the people at
large. To the extent this judgement was valid, it raised
serious doubts about the solidity of any U.S. entente with
Pakistan. Actually, Pakistan had been facing for some time
a crisis of political legitimacy and national integration which
military rule had not been able to resolve.
　　Central to the crisis of legitimacy is the unresolved tension
between authoritarianism and popular demand for democracy. What is unique about Pakistan is not the military's
intervention in politics—which had occurred in 1958, 1969,
1971 and 1977—but the consistency of public resistance to
such rule. The cyle of resistance and suppression has pro-

gressively widened the gap between popular aspirations and political power. After independence in 1947, the early deaths of Mohammed Ali Jinnah, Pakistan's founding father, and of his deputy, Liaquat Ali Khan, deprived the country of the foremost leaders deemed capable of investing democratic institutions with real power. National power shifted to the army and bureaucracy, whose strength was vastly augmented by a military alliance with the United States. Manipulation and suppression of representative institutions followed and included the arbitrary dismissal in 1954 of Pakistan's first elected government in East Pakistan.

In 1958, General Mohammed Ayub Khan overthrew the parliamentary regime. Popular uprisings in 1968-69 for representative government led to Ayub's overthrow. The elections held in 1970 under the military were free but were frustrated in 1971 by military intervention in East Pakistan, which led to the country's dismemberment and defeat at the hands of India. Military rule was discredited, and the mood among the soldiers favored a return to the barracks.

Following the disastrous defeat that brought the amputation of East Pakistan, Zulfikar Ali Bhutto, a fiery but urbane politician who had served his country abroad in a number of diplomatic posts, was elected president. Bhutto's failure to exploit this opportunity did not bode well for democratic rule. He was voted to power after promising reforms and democracy. Yet he forced out the elected state governments of Baluchistan and the Northwest Frontier Province; banned the main opposition party, the National Awami Party; provoked armed insurrection in Baluchistan and ordered military intervention there. Finally, with thousands of his opponents in prison, rigged elections were held in 1977. He admitted that rigging had occurred but denied its magnitude; disclaiming responsibility, he rejected popular demands for new elections and called out the army to suppress mass protests. His imposition of martial law in major cities, in disregard of a court injunction against it as being unconstitutional, set the stage for the restoration of the military as the extra-constitutional arbiter of Pakistani politics.

After ousting Bhutto, the generals proclaimed themselves a caretaker government, promising to restore constitutional rule within ninety days. The promised return to democratic government did not take place. When the military government finally did agree to hold elections in November 1979, two years after it seized power, it went back on its word. In October of that year, General Zia, in a radio address to the nation, announced that he had postponed indefinitely the following month's elections, banned all political parties and meetings, outlawed strikes, closed some newspapers and magazines and imposed censorship on the rest. These stringent measures were necessary, Zia declared, because he did not believe that elections would lead to a stable government. "No one can be allowed to destroy the country in the name of democracy," he went on, "nor will violence be permitted in the name of politics." The president, who had proclaimed martial law on seizing power, announced that "martial law hereafter will be what martial law should be."

Closely linked to the question of democracy is the issue of provincial autonomy and the right of important minorities in Pakistan to control their own local affairs. Successive governments have failed to deal with this explosive issue, including that of General Zia. As long as this problem remains unresolved, it was argued, full national integration would elude the country; the issue, thereby, threatened Pakistan's territorial integrity and very political existence. An alliance with a country having such deep-rooted problems will necessarily pose serious political risks for the United States. Conceivably, such an entente could unravel in the same way as relations with Iran following the overthrow of the shah and the establishment of a revolutionary Islamic government in Teheran.

Pakistan has been dominated since its inception by its majority linguistic group, the Punjabis, who make up approximately sixty percent of the population. This Punjabi predominance is bitterly resented by the other three major groups, the Baluchis, the Pushtuns and the Sindhis, whose ancestral homelands account for seventy-two percent of Pakistan territory. All three groups contend with varying degrees of justice that they are excluded from their fair share of political and economic power by a Punjabi-dominated military and bureaucratic elite. Some influential leaders among all three groups have been arguing in terms of secession from Pakistan and have been exploring the possibilities for winning independence with foreign help, whether from the Soviet Union, the Arab world, India or the West. The preponderance of evidence on this count is that most of the leaders are fighting for democratic rights within Pakistan at both the provincial and national levels.

Separatist sentiment has been strong in the strategically located Baluchi area, which has a 750-mile coastline stretching along the Arabian Sea across western Pakistan and eastern Iran directly to the south of Afghanistan. Baluchi nationalist factions have long dreamed of a "Greater Baluchistan" that would unite the five million Baluchis in Pakistan and Iran. Should an independent Baluchistan come into existence under Soviet auspices, Moscow would have ready naval access to the Persian Gulf and would gain a new position of leverage along Iran's eastern flank.

In the case of the Pushtuns, separatist feeling is rooted in the fact that the Pushtun population of fourteen million is divided almost equally between Pakistan and contiguous areas of Afghanistan. Pushtun dynasties in Kabul ruled a united Pushtun kingdom, encompassing most of what is now northern Pakistan, until the British raj pushed back the Afghan boundary to the Khyber Pass little more than a century ago. More recently, Kabul, encouraged by Moscow, has periodically promoted a movement for an Afghan-controlled "Pushtunistan" to be carved out of the Pakistani Pushtun area. This movement has been eclipsed by the

Afghan war, but it could well be revived if the Soviet-backed Babrak Karmal regime stabilizes its military and political position.

The most acute of these problems is the situation in Baluchistan, whose 134,000 square miles make it Pakistan's largest province although having the fewest people—2.5 million. Baluchis have insisted that their bitterness is rooted in neglect by the Punjabis. Baluchistan's natural resources, such as natural gas, coal, onyx and marble are shipped elsewhere in the country, mainly to Punjab and Sind provinces. Little development aid has been brought into the sparsely populated and barren province. Although Baluchis rail against the economic neglect of their province, tribal leaders are most vocal about years of political repression. It was President Bhutto's threat to their political power that made them take up arms against the central government. They wanted aid but on the condition that the government bestow it on the chiefs so that they could deliver it to the people. Bhutto took his aid directly to the people while the army attempted to destroy the power of the chiefs.

Pakistan's Baluchistan problem arose in earnest in 1973 when local candidates of the National Awami League swept the provincial elections. President Bhutto responded by declaring the league illegal. Consistent with his aim of breaking the power of the local chiefs, Bhutto had over seven hundred of them jailed or placed under house arrest. While the army razed villages of rebellious tribesmen, thousands went into exile in Afghanistan. There are reports that anywhere from five hundred to five thousand Baluchis are still there, receiving training in insurgency from Soviet and Afghan advisers. After Zia assumed power and ordered Bhutto executed, he granted an amnesty to the Baluchi dissidents. Despite this, he has refused to grant them the autonomy they seek and democratic rights.

Confronted by the specter of a possible Soviet push southward toward the Arabian Sea, the United States clearly has an interest in promoting a more democratic and stable Pakistan capable of dealing effectively with separatist tendencies. But the U.S. dilemma is that the Punjabi-dominated Zia ul-Huq regime has so far failed to take even minimal economic and political measures needed to accomodate these tendencies in the Baluchi, as well as the Pushtun areas. Many of the acknowledged political leaders in these areas are reportedly still prepared for an accommodation with Islamabad. The essential precondition for significant inputs of U.S. military aid to Pakistan, it is suggested, should, therefore, be an interim political settlement between the central government and the Baluchi and Pushtun moderates. Given a meaningful devolution of power and resources, observers assert, Islamabad would have powerful local allies in these two disaffected areas whose cooperation would be essential in mobilizing any effective tribal support for the Pakistan military in the event of Soviet-supported separatist adventures. In the absence of a settlement, there is the strong likelihood that U.S. weapons would be used not against Soviet-supported subversion but against Baluchi and Pushtun dissident groups fighting for what they regard as their legitimate rights as Pakistanis. During the inconclusive guerrilla war in Baluchistan between 1973 and 1977, the Pakistani Air Force used U.S.-supplied helicopters to raze Baluchi villages indiscriminately.

The military, however, is described as ill-suited to promote a settlement that could lead to integration. Status and privilege accrue to members of the military, yet Baluchis and Sindhis have negligible representation in it; eighty percent are Punjabis, largely from a few rural districts. For the non-Punjabis, forty-two percent of the country's population, the army symbolizes inequality and Punjabi domination. The generals' preference for a strong centralized government causes deep anxiety in the minority provinces, which are said to regard a federal, parliamentary system as the best for redressing their grievances.

U.S. Policy & the Security of the Gulf

In his State of the Union address to the Congress in January 1980, President Carter brought to the fore an aspect of American foreign policy that had generally not been well understood by the public. It had to do with the importance of the Persian Gulf to American and Western interests and the need for protecting this area against external aggression.

In pledging to use American power to repel external aggression in the Gulf, President Carter was enunciating a new statement of policy. According to this position, the United States was prepared to assume primary military responsibility. This constituted a major shift in policy, which in the past had assigned primary responsibility for the defense of the Gulf to Iran and Saudi Arabia. This had been the so-called "two-pillar" policy that had evolved under the Nixon Doctrine. This doctrine was based on the organization of client-states into American-sponsored military pacts. The client-state system blossomed at the height of the Cold War when Secretary of State John Foster Dulles fashioned an interlocking set of regional pacts that was meant to halt the spread of communism. While the utility of these pacts was called into question a decade later during the war in Vietnam, the American debacle in Indochina also had the effect of underscoring the dangers of direct military intervention in regional conflicts. Under the so-called Nixon Doctrine of the early 1970s, client states in critical regions took on greater responsibility in American strategic planning. In the Persian Gulf, defense of the region fell to the two major friendly regional powers, namely, Iran and Saudi Arabia. This is now changing, with the U.S. assuming the role that had previously been played by these two so-called "regional influentials."

U.S. Policy & Gulf Security: Pre-Khomeini

The Persian Gulf/Arabian Peninsula area is made up of ten countries that are related geographically, religiously and, for the most part, ethnically but that present sharp and distinctive economic and political contrasts. Some have long histories as independent nations with established interests and influence in and beyond the area, while others have achieved independence as recently as 1971. All have strong economic ties with the outside world. Several, notably Saudi Arabia and Kuwait, are among the world's wealthiest in terms of per capita GNP, while others, such as the Republic of Yemen, are classed among the poorest. Their political systems range from absolute monarchy based on Koranic law through gradations of parliamentary democracy to a Marxist-Leninist-style "people's republic." Except for the People's Democratic Republic of Yemen, where the United States has had no diplomatic relations and no official presence since October 1969, and Iraq, where despite the absence of diplomatic relations Washington maintains a small U.S. Interest Section in the Belgian embassy, American relations with all the countries in the region have been good. With many of the countries, the depth and variety of these relations have grown significantly in recent years.

United States relations with the countries in the region have to be understood against a background of spectacular changes, the most important of which are the following:

•New political institutions have been formed and tested, and traditional societies are undergoing rapid change. Among these changes are rapid urbanization, breakdown of traditional tribal ties and, in certain countries, the emergence of some of the trappings of an advanced economy based on strong ties to the West.

•A dramatic evolution has taken place in the production and pricing of the region's most import commodity, oil. This power is now effectively lodged with OPEC, in which Saudi Arabia, Iran, Kuwait and Iraq have a preponderant voice. The international oil companies, notably the Arabian American Oil Co. (ARAMCO), have either been bought out or nationalized or operate under close control of the host government.

•There has been an accelerating transfer of technology from the West to the Gulf states. To judge from the experience in Iran, where this transfer took place at a frenzied pace with only limited results in modernizing the country, it would be premature to assess the effectiveness of this transfer and its impact on the people as a whole. The oil-producing states have been diversifying and industrializing their economies as part of a strategy to modernize society and to create new assets to take the place of oil when it will no longer be available.

•Since Britain's termination of its protective treaty relationship with a number of the Gulf states, there has been a discernible effort toward greater regional cooperation in promoting peace in the region. One of the consequences of the overthrow of the shah has been to arrest, if not reverse, this trend.

It is against this background, that one can better appreciate U.S. foreign policy objectives in the region. These objectives were succinctly stated by Under Secretary of State for Political Affairs Joseph J. Sisco before the Special

Subcommittee on Investigations of the Committee on International Relations of the House of Representatives in June 1975. These policies, established in the anticipation of the British departure from the region in 1971, were:

•Support for collective security and stability in the region by encouraging indigenous regional cooperative efforts and orderly economic progress.

•Making available military equipment and training services to allow the countries to meet their legitimate defense requirements.

•Continued access to the region's oil supplies at reasonable prices and in sufficient quantities to meet U.S. needs and those of its allies.

•Expansion of U.S. diplomatic, cultural, technical commercial and financial presence.

•Assistance to oil exporters to employ their rapidly growing incomes in a constructive way, supportive of the international financial system.

The Soviet invasion of Afghanistan was immediately interpreted in Washington as a direct threat to U.S. interests in the Persian Gulf. Since World War II, the United States had developed a Persain Gulf strategy that centered on and around Iran. It had not been the first country to do so.

Long before oil became a key factor in international politics, Iran had attracted the attention of imperial states. What gives it such strategic importance is that it is located south of the Caucasus and the Caspian Sea (i.e., south of a line from Batum to Baku) and blocks Russian access to the warm waters of the Persian Gulf and the Indian Ocean. It also lies astride the easiest land route from the northwest into the Indian subcontinent. This explains why Napoleon foresaw a role for Iran in his grandiose scheme to conquer British India—thwarted by Nelson at the battle of the Nile in 1798. It explains the 19th century rivalry over Iran between Victorian Britain and the Russia of the czars. The British always suspected the Russians of having designs on their Indian empire. It also explains why the Eastern Front in World War I spilled over into northeastern Iran.

The commissars, like the czars, had no less an apprecia-
tion of Iran's strategic importance. In 1940, while Nazi
Germany and communist Russia were linked by a non-
aggression pact, the Soviet leadership spelled out quite
clearly how it perceived Iran. Then Soviet Foreign Minister
Vyacheslav Molotov submitted to the German ambassador
in Moscow—with a view to Hitler's eventual approval—a
draft proposal to the effect "that the area south of Batum
and Baku in the general direction of the Persian Gulf is
recognized as the center of the aspirations of the Soviet
Union." The Nazi dictator subsequently balked at this, and
the Nazi-Soviet pact, which had helped precipitate the
Second World War, began to unravel.

Not long after Hitler invaded the Soviet Union, Stalin
joined with Winston Churchill, England's wartime leader, in
occupying Iran. Their aim was to block the Nazi thrust
toward the Caucasus both from outflanking the Soviet
armies and from lunging at the British in India; no less
important was the need to establish a secure route to channel
war supplies to the Russians. On taking over Iran, the Allies
forced Riza Shah, a German sympathizer, to abdicate; his
son, Mohammed Riza Pahllvi, then 22, took power. After
the war, Stalin attempted to stay on by establishing puppet
regimes in Azerbaijan and Kurdistan, two of Iran's most
populous non-Persian provinces. The Soviets backed away
from this plan after President Truman served notice on the
Kremlin that the United States would not tolerate the parti-
tion of Iran.

U.S.-Iranian Relations Under the Shah

That Iran emerged as the foremost power in the Persian
Gulf was, as already noted, largely a consequence of President Nixon's decision in 1969 to assign it a key role in the
region.

Nixon's action was prompted by Prime Minister Harold
Wilson's decision in 1968 to withdraw the last of British
troops from the Far East and the Persian Gulf by 1971. At

the urging of Secretary of State Kissinger, Nixon agreed that the task of policing the Gulf be handed over to Iran. It should not be overlooked that the shah was eager to assume such a role. He was anxious to transform his country into the major power in the region.

To give expression to this policy, Washington agreed to build up Iran as a military power; in exchange, Teheran agreed to serve as the "guardian and protector" of the West's oil supplies. The staff of a Senate Foreign Relations subcommittee reported that President Nixon in 1972 decided to "sell Iran virtually any conventional weapons it wanted." In May 1972, Nixon and Kissinger flew to Teheran to seal this new U.S.-Iranian partnership. The decision to arm Iran was a corollary that followed from the "Nixon Doctrine." Under this doctrine, Iran and Saudi Arabia as well were to become pivotal client-states for the defence of the Gulf. Overextended in Southeast Asia, the U.S. was in no position to police the Gulf by itself. Iran was permitted to acquire the necessary weapons to serve as surrogate for Washington.

The quadrupling of oil prices in 1973-1974 allowed the shah to buy weapons from the United States on a scale that few could have anticipated when the agreement was first consumated. Between 1972 and 1978, Iran ordered $19.5 billion worth of arms. One U.S. Congressman called it "the most rapid military build-up of military power under peacetime conditions of any nation in the history of the world." It was not long before the shah asserted this newly acquired military strength. At the invitation of the sultan of Oman, he sent troops to crush a South Yemeni-backed rebellion in Dhofar province. In the Persian Gulf, the shah's air force and navy were active in guaranteeing freedom of navigation in this vital waterway and in keeping open the Straits of Hormuz. In order to run and maintain this vast arsenal, more than 20,000 Americans, military and civilian, poured into the country. The Iranian forces were so dependent on American personnel to assist them that the staff of a Senate Foreign Relations subcommittee concluded that Iran could

not wage war "without U.S. support on a day-to-day basis."
This view was supported by the little rebellion of Kurds that
Iran stirred up in neighboring Iraq. The shah had to aban-
don the fight in 1975 after his forces were repulsed.

With strong encouragement from Washington, Saudi
Arabia became a partner in the Nixon-Kissinger east-of-
Suez strategy, dubbed the "two-pillar" policy. No less than
Iran, oil-rich Saudi Arabia provided a tempting target to
radical forces in the region, particularly Soviet-aligned
South Yemen to the south. And like the Iranians, the Saudis
have spent lavishly in creating a modern military establishment with American arms. Riyadh's primary role in the
region, however, had been to use its vast financial resources
to shore up moderate governments in and around the Persian Gulf and Red Sea. Financial aid has been doled out to
Oman, South Yemen, North Yemen, Bahrain and Egypt
(now withdrawn). In the conflict-ridden Horn of Africa, the
Saudis held out the lure of money to pry the leftist government of Somalia away from its alliance with the Soviets; in
1978, the Somali government, outraged over Soviet backing
for its arch enemy Ethiopia, expelled the Russians from the
bases it had provided them under a treaty agreement with
Moscow.

Iran's security role in the Gulf, complemented by Saudi
Arabia, gave concrete meaning to the "two pillar" policy.
Viewed from the U.S. vantage point, this application of the
"Nixon Doctrine" proved its worth. Western access to the
oil fields remained undisturbed and the Soviets were kept at
arms length. Iran, whose position gave every indication of
being bolstered by the American connection, became the
pivotal member of CENTO, at a time when its two other
members, Turkey and Pakistan, were wracked by internal
tension.

In military, economic and foreign affairs—at least since
the early 1960s—the shah sought to maintain "a primary but
not confining alignment with the United States." This was
the description of William E. Griffith of the Massachusetts

Institute of Technology, and there is much in the record to support it. The shah bought British Chieftain tanks to replace American models. He sought French as well as American nuclear plants. He even bought some lesser weapons such as artillery from the Soviet Union. In 1962, he signed an agreement with Moscow promising that no United States missiles would be stationed in Iran, with which the Russians share a 1,2000-mile border. On the other hand, he allowed the United States to maintain listening posts in Iran to monitor Soviet missile development.

Sometimes, the shah used Washington rather than the other way around. This was particularly true in matters relating to political developments in the Persian Gulf region. For example, he took the initiative and urged President Nixon to weaken radical Iraq by supplying arms for a Kurdish uprising in 1974. As an added twist, the Kurds were given Soviet weapons captured by Israel, a fact that must have stunned the pro-Soviet Iraqis who captured them. That the venture turned out badly had more to do with the ineffectiveness of the Iranian army than the weakness of the plan. Far and away the most consequential show of independence by the shah was his successful push to drive up oil prices from 1973 on. Probably no single set of circumstances has done more to mire the West in the inflation-stagnation rut in which it has languished ever since. At meetings of OPEC, Saudi Arabia has been pictured as a "moderate." It could afford to be; it has not been trying to earn billions of dollars for outsized industries and armies. But the shah's ambitions were loftier. So his ministers, sometimes with Venezuela, led the charge for the increases that have hit the U.S. economy with great force. Clearly, this was not the way one would expect a puppet to behave.

Although a hawk on oil prices, the shah maintained oil production at the continuous high level of 6.5 million barrels a day. This assured an ample world supply while keeping periodic OPEC price increases within bounds. The importance of this high level of production came to be fully appreciated in the West following the shah's overthrow. At that time, Iranian production dropped dramatically and set in motion the escalation of oil prices throughtout 1979, resulting in a 150-percent price increase. The shah, more-over,never attached political conditions to the sale of oil, which flowed uninterruptedly to the West during the 1973 Arab oil embargo. During the 1973 Yom Kippur War, the shah continued to sell oil to Israel despite strong Arab efforts to dissuade him.

Sino-Iranian Relations

As part of his efforts to play a leading role on the world diplomatic stage, the shah courted the People's Republic of China. An astute diplomat, it was said, he realized that good ties with Peking could serve as a counterweight to the Soviets. Even before the Nixon opening to China, the shah sent his twin sister, Princess Ashraf, to Peking in April 1971; Empress Farah, the shah's wife, followed a year later.

Friendship with China meant that Iran could be on good terms with the three great powers. Such a relationship had solid practical dimensions. It could serve as a hedge against Soviet intrigues in the region. Since the Marxist coup in Afghanistan in April 1978, both Iran and China had added reason to be concerned about Soviet activity in this country. Afghanistan, which has common borders with Iran and China, could, at the behest of the Soviet Union, stir up Baluchi dissidents. Baluchistan overlaps areas of Afghani-stan, Iran and Pakistan (which maintains close ties with China), and a separatist movement there could provide Moscow with an opening wedge into this area.

The Chinese, who know history, have shown an acute understanding of Iran's key role in all the great power conflicts of the past couple of centuries. In the summer of 1978, Chinese Communist party leader Hua Kuo-feng made

Iran one of the three stops on his first journey westward
outside China; Romania and Yugoslavia were the other two.
This was evidence that Peking recognized Iran's role in any
containment of the Soviet Union. This was the first visit ever
of a chairman of the People's Republic of China to a non-
communist country. The reasons the Chinese had for court-
ing the shah, much to the disgust of Iranian dissidents and
liberals in Third World countries, were clear enough. Peking
was clearly troubled over Soviet gains in Afghanistan and
the possible threat this posed to China's long-time Pakistani
allies. Chairman Hua's visit and the growing ties to Iran
were designed to outflank these gains.

Iranian-Israeli Relations

One of the shah's policies that earned him much dislike in
the Arab world was his consistently good ties with Israel.
Although officially neutral in the Arab-Israel conflict, for
which he favored a diplomatic settlement, he had been
supportive of the Jewish state in a number of important
areas. In 1950, the shah extended *de facto* recognition to the
Jewish state; when he reaffirmed this position ten years
later, it provoked a hostile reaction from Egyptian President
Nasser, who broke diplomatic relations with Teheran.
Friendly relations with this Islamic but non-Arabic state
provided Israel with an important haven to operate economically and diplomatically on the Arab world's eastern edge.

Two matters of importance brought Iran and Israel
together: oil and security. All other facets of their relationship stemmed from these two paramount concerns, which
are opposite aides of the same coin. A reliable source of oil is
a necessary condition of survival for Israel, which has virtually no important sources of energy. The shah demonstrated
friendship for Israel in the 1967 and 1973 wars by keeping
the oil flowing. The oil nexus had provided Israel with
enormous economic as well as political benefits. Without

the pledge of an uninterrupted flow of oil, Israel would not have built the $150 million pipeline between Eilat and Ashdod along with concomitant investments in port facilities, supertankers and a refinery in Ashkelon. The flow of oil stopped with the coming to power of the Islamic government of the Ayatollah Khomeini.

Historically, the shah's policy toward Israel was rooted in the assumption that a militarily strong and economically viable Jewish state could serve as an effective countervailing force to the expansionist tendencies of Arab nationalism. The persistence of the Arab-Israeli struggle, along with the perennial inter-Arab rivalries, it was reasoned, would absorb energies that might otherwise be directed toward the Persian Gulf. One of Nasser's objectives was to gain hegemony in this strategic region. Iraq, too, it was feared, given a chance, might have similar aims. Nasser had made no secret of his desire to gain access to this great wealth to finance his own revolution in Egypt and the Arab world. Following his cue, Arabs began referring to the Persian Gulf as the Arabian Gulf and to oil-rich Khuzistan, a majority of whose population is Arab, as Arabistan.

Following the six-day war of 1967, the shah moved to improve his ties with the Arabs, notably Egypt and Saudi Arabia. At the same time Teheran cautiously supported the Palestinians. In the United Nations, the Iranian delegation spoke out in favor of resolutions calling for a return of the Palestinian people to Palestine, for recognition of the Palestine Liberation Organization (PLO) as the sole legitimate representative of the Palestinian people, and for granting it observer status in the world organization. Iran did not, however, identify with the Arab position of calling in question Israel's right to exist. Much of Iran's support was rhetorical and did not translate into material support for the PLO. The latter was deeply suspect in the Iranian court, which had reason to believe that Iranian dissidents of all political stripes were receiving guerrilla training in PLO camps. Indeed, after the shah's overthrow, Yasir Arafat, the leader of the PLO, was the first political leader to be welcomed to Teheran by the Ayatollah Khomeini.

Iranian-Arab Relations

There were several interrelated factors that accounted for the shift in Iranian policy toward the Arab world, mainly the more moderate Arab countries. Following Egypt's defeat in the war of 1967, Iran had little to fear from this Arab state, the most powerful in the Arab world. Nothing more was heard of Egyptian ambitions in the Persian Gulf. This shift in policy, begun in the last years of the Nasser regime, was continued by his successor, President Anwar Sadat. Diplomatic relations between Cairo and Teheran were restored in 1970. Abandoning Nasser's police of hostility toward King Faisal, the pragmatic Egyptian leader courted the oil-rich Arab monarch and made friendship with Saudi Arabia the cornerstone of his policies in the Arab world. Having been drawn into this conservative political orbit, it was only natural that Sadat make his peace with the shah as well. Except for the radical Arab states, most of the others followed the Egyptian lead and cultivated friendlier ties with the shah, whose stock in the Arab world was rising.

Iran's efforts to promote good ties with its Arab neighbors were also a consequence of the shah's policy of becoming the preeminent regional power in the Gulf. He and King Khalid of Saudi Arabia had common interests in maintaining stability in the Gulf. Much the same reason prompted the shah to improve relations with Iraq, whose close ties to the Soviets and radical politics were seen as a threat to the conservative political leaders who ruled throughout the Gulf. In 1975, the two countries ended their long feud by negotiating an accord in Algiers under which the Iraqis agreed to modify the boundary line in the Shatt 'al Arab estuary in Iran's favor in exchange for the shah's ending his support of the Kurdish rebellion in northern Iraq.

Iraq, Iran and Saudi Arabia undertook joint discussions in 1978 as part of an effort to form a security alliance. The willingness of Baghdad to even discuss such an agreement with Iran and Saudi Arabia reflected a growing estrangement between Iraq and the Soviets. The Iraqis, along with the other two Persian Gulf states, had become increasingly concerned over the growing Soviet involvement in the Horn of Africa and in Afghanistan. Although Baghdad continued its treaty ties with Moscow and continued to acquire arms from it, there were distinct signs of a cooling in relations. Iraq undertook a policy of developing closer economic links with the West and the U.S. even though it had no diplomatic ties with Washington. Instead of relying mainly on the Soviets for arms, Iraq began to diversify its sources of arms purchases. Internally, the government took a hard line against the communist party, accusing it of attempting to penetrate the army with organized cells.

Revolution in Iran

In the fall of 1978, the widespread unrest in Iran took on all the characteristics of a thorough-going revolution against the 37-year rule of the shah. In that year there were violent confrontations between the shah's opponents and the three paramilitary forces responsible for domestic security—the Iranian Ground Forces, the National Police and the Gendarmerie. The shah installed his chief of staff, General Gholamreza Ashari, as Prime Minister in early November as a last resort—an attempt, according to the monarch, to gain time for a peaceful transition to a freely elected civilian government.

In his bid to maintain his once-unquestioned power, the shah received strong backing from President Carter and from Hua Kuo-feng, China's premier and party leader. Soviet leaders had also quietly agreed that political chaos to the south would be inimical to their interests.

Despite this diplomatic support and the vast array of military power at his disposal, the shah was unable to save his throne. A combination of Islamic-inspired opposition and left-wing elements forced the shah to leave the country. The undisputed victor was the Ayatollah Khomeini, who, more than anyone else, mobilized the masses of the Iranian people to overthrow what was widely regarded as a hated regime.

Opposition to the shah's rule was rooted in a number of factors. The heart of the complaint was that the shah ran the country as a personal fiefdom, slaughtering demonstrators, torturing and killing suspected enemies, pilfering the nation's wealth, overturning and corrupting traditional values and handing control of the country over to the United States. There have been repeated findings by respected international bodies that the shah treated suspected dissidents ruthlessly. He himself acknowledged as much, telling the Italian journalist Oriana Fallaci: "Believe me, when three-quarters of a nation doesn't know how to read, you can provide for reforms only by the strictest authoritarianism—otherwise you get nowhere." It is much harder, however, to conclude that he had been a puppet dangling at the end of a string pulled in Washington; he frequently thwarted U.S. objectives, not least in leading the drive for higher oil prices. Among the major charges against the shah and his rule:

Massacre of the population. Starting in January 1978 in the holy city of Qum, demonstrations against the shah spread through the country like a burning fuse, to Tabriz, Isfahan, smaller towns, to Teheran itself. Almost everywhere, soldiers fired on the crowds, who seemed almost to ignore the bullets. The toll is a matter of dispute. The International Institute of Strategic Studies, a private research group with good Western intelligence sources, reported the total as "at least 2,000." Iranian President Abolhassan Bani-Sadr estimated that the shah "has probably killed more than 100,000 people" in the last fifteen years of his rule.

Torture of dissidents & political opponents. The International Commission of Jurists, a respected Geneva-based private group, reported in 1976 that: "There is abundant evidence showing the systematic use of impermissible methods of psychological and physical torture of political suspects during interrogation." That year Amnesty International, both a private group and a Noble laureate, published a study charging Iran with arbitrary arrests of suspected political opponents, torture and unaccounted deaths. A year earlier, Amnesty International had concluded that "the torture of political prisoners during interrogation appears to be a routine practice." The agency observed that the shah had been accused of holding 25,000 to 100,000 prisoners, but no reliable number could be cited. The regime typically acknowledged about 3,000.

These broad summaries connot capture the feel of what it was said to be like in the torture chambers of the shah. Riza Baraheni, an Iranian novelist arrested in1973, provided this description of the double, iron-bed technique: "They tie you to the upper bed on your back, and with the heat coming from torch or a small heater, they burn your back in order to extract information. Sometimes the burning is extended to the spine, as a result of which paralysis is certain." Baraheni saw and experienced other things. "There were also all sizes of whips hanging from nails on the walls. Electric prods stood on little stools. The nail-plucking instruments stood on the far side. The gallows stood on the other side. They hang you upside down and then someone beats you with a club on your legs or uses the electric prod on your chest or genitals, or they lower you down, pull your pants up and one of them tries to rape you while you are still hanging upside down." These charges of torture were far from unique and help explain the groundswell of emotion against the shah who, it was widely believed, was not ignorant about what was going on inside the chambers of SAVAK, the hated and feared secret service.

Plunder of public funds & assets. The shah and his family were undoubtedly rich, but how much legitimately belonged to them and how much they had improperly hidden are impossible to determine. Budgeting in Iran was more feudal than modern, with no firm distinction between revenues for the state and income to the shah. There was no way of fixing a proper salary for such a ruler or estimating what its investment might yield. It is just as hard to determine how much wealth the shah and his family have acquired. Officials of the revolutionary regime put it as high as thirty billion dollars. The shah had reportedly told a friend, Barbara Walters, the television reporter, that it ranged from fifty million to a hundred million dollars, a differential that in itself suggests accounting of a most informal sort. The Pahlevi Foundation, which he controlled, was thought to have assets of about three billion dollars, with shares in big banks, cement plants, insurance companies, sugar mills, casinos, a General Motors plant and twenty-five percent of the Krupp steel works in West Germany. According to some authorities, every new enterprise set up in Iran gave the shah or his relatives a small share. Many arms deals were sealed only with the payment of a "commission" to an Iranian middleman who, it is assumed, shared his windfall with the shah. In light of the reportedly vast amount of wealth that the shah and his family took for themselves, the revolutionary authorities in Teheran had demanded the return of this wealth as a condition for releasing the American embassy hostages. This had become one of the major issues between the U.S. and the revolutionary regime.

Inspired decadence and secularization. The shah viewed himself as a modernizer, single-handedly lifting a traditional, rural Muslim country into the 20th century. He bought nuclear plants from the United States and France, he built an international airline, he gave women the vote, he permitted male and female students to ride on the same buses and eat in the same cafeterias, he brought in movies and casinos and choked his captial with cars.

Above all, industry secularizes, breaks down the attachment to traditional religious values. The religious establishment, now personified by the Ayatollah Khomeini, was resentful. Even the shah's redistribution of land struck directly at the mullahs, depriving them of the generous bequests that had made them rich in land. Their primitive network of welfare for the poor was superseded by jobs in booming industry and the social measures the shah undertook. Civil courts replaced those run by the mullahs. The emancipation of women, the prostitutes drawn to the boom towns, all were an affront to their power and beliefs. The mob swirling around the American embassy was described as "a rallying cry against excessive and indiscriminate Westernization, in part a protest against the erosion of traditional values."

Misguided & mismanaged economic development. As economists measure economic development, the shah had presided over an economic miracle, even before the great boom in oil prices. In the dozen years to 1972, the output of goods and services grew at an astonishing 9.4 per cent a year. With the quadrupling of oil prices, growth increased tremendously. The gross national product leaped thirty-four per cent in 1974, forty-two per cent in 1975. Income per head skyrocketed from $176 in 1960 to $1,997 in 1976, although inflation ate into much these gains.

To be sure, the distribution of this new wealth was unequal. Half the nation lived in the countryside, and nine of ten were housed in mud-brick huts. At least half of the people in overcrowded Teheran also made their homes in twisted lanes lined with mud-brick dwellings. An estimated ten per cent of the population owned forty per cent of the wealth. Young men poured into the cities from a countryside that was neglected. They flocked to projects and plants that were built by big companies from the United States, Great Britain, France and other industrial countries. Bottlenecks soon developed in elaborate plans for factories, superhighways and a subway in Teheran. Inflation reached nearly fifty per cent. Credits had to be squeezed. Projects creaked to a halt before they could turn out an offsetting stream of goods to match the demand from the hundreds of thousands of workers and others enjoying high paper incomes. The collapse of the boom and the jobless this created almost surely helped inspire the demonstrators who howled for the overthrow of the shah and applauded the seizure of the American hostages.

The shah's economic strategy was to develop Iran into a major industrial power by the end of the twentieth century. In this rush to industrialize, huge sums were invested in a wide range of urban-based enterprises. Foreign capital was encouraged to invest in Iran. As a result of this policy, the economy became distorted, and what passed for development became an engine for political discontent. Much of the goods that were produced could be purchased by a relatively small segment of the population. The vast army of young people, largely men, who migrated to Teheran and a few other large cities, earned too little to acquire the goods and services that the massive investment yielded. The shah's economic advisers neglected the all-important agricultural sector. Thus, Iran, once an exporter of food, had to import basic food commodities to cover its food requirements. Foreign exchange that could have been used to purchase needed in-puts for agriculture was increasingly diverted to buy the very food that Iran could have produced. Even the well-intentioned land reform program of the early sixties turned out to be something of a disaster. Farmers were not given credits to buy fertilizer, pesticides and other needs. Acquiring title to land was an insufficient basis for a farmer to become self-sufficient and gradually produce for commercial markets. As a result, many farmers were forced to sell their land, flocking to the cities in search of jobs in the rapidly mushrooming industrial and housing sectors. When these sectors collapsed in 1977-78 for want of credit and markets, the disgruntled unemployed turned on the shah and the system he created.

Political dictatorship. The shah came to power in 1941 through foreign intervention. In 1953, when nationalist forces under Dr. Mohammed Mossadegh succeeded in ousting the shah and seizing the British-run oil fields, the U.S.' Central Intelligence Agency restored him to power. Kermit Roosevelt, the grandson of Theodore Roosevelt, was the official in the CIA who organized this counter-coup.

Gradually, the young ruler shook off the feeling of dependency that became associated with these foreign forces. In time he established an unchallenged dictatorial rule by breaking all forms of domestic opposition, notably that of the mullahs, whose land he expropriated in the 1960s for distribution to the peasants. Dictatorial rule became increasingly irrelevant to the needs of a rapidly modernizing state. The newly created middle class and urban workers who were benefitting from the system were not brought into the political structure which made decisions that more and more affected their lives and fortune. This failure to establish political institutions to involve the people in the political process has been described as a fatal mistake for the shah. The beneficiaries of his economic system turned on him at the moment he would need their support. The women of Iran, to whom he gave the vote and whom he freed from the constraints of traditional Islamic society, also would not support him; the ballot was meaningless to them in the absence of true democracy, and their Westernization had a hollow ring to it within the larger Muslim society, which remained untouched by the reforms. Politically, the shah was often described as a cruel and inept leader who believed that he alone could guide Iran into the twentieth century. He was called an authoritarian leader who failed to comprehend the needs of his people for political freedom as well as economic progress. However, it should be kept in mind, his authoritarian rule was in keeping with history and the country's traditional political practices. One of the informed verdicts on the shah comes from Robert Graham, a British journalist whose *Iran: The Illusion of Power* was written on the eve of the monarch's downfall. Graham wrote:

"To cast the Shah as the villain is in one sense misleading. There is nothing to suggest that another leader or group of leaders in Iran would have done better or behaved much differently under the circumstances. It would be surprising if the same basic motivations did not apply; namely the preservation of personal power, a concern with prestige, chauvinistic pride in seeking Iranian solutions, and a general impatience with detail. The Shah's critics decry his authoritarianism, but there is scarcely a liberal tradition in Iranian history. Even Mossadegh in his brief experience of power dismissed Parliament and displayed a penchant for authoritarian rule."

The Last Days of the Shah

In the hour of his greatest peril, the last months of 1978, the shah, already ill with the cancer that in little more than a year would cause his death, was constantly assured of Washington's support. On November 30, President Carter said: "We have confidence in the shah. We support him and his efforts to change Iran in a constructive way." Twelve days later, the President said at another news conference that Iran's leader "has our support and he also has our confidence."

At that stage, such verbal support carried little weight; the lines of support that had once existed had long ago frayed. There were no Kermit Roosevelts or forces of an even larger order to protect the huge American investment in the shah's regime. The reality is said to be that the Carter Administration not only proved unable to save the shah but actually contributed to the collapse of his regime by sending conflicting policy signals that demoralized him and his armed forces. When President Carter failed to impose a clear policy line on his quarreling advisers, the ensuing confusion encouraged anti-shah forces and bewildered the shah, already weakened by drugs prescribed for his cancer, according to an article published in the *Washington Quarterly*. (The journal is published by Georgetown University's Center for Strategic Studies, a conservative think-tank whose members include former high government officials such as Henry Kissinger and James Schlesinger.)

In the article, "Carter and the Fall of the Shah: the Inside Story," writers Michael Ledeen and William Lewis argue that the U.S. Administration was consistently overconfident about the Iranian military's ability to intervene to forestall the impending revolution. Referring to what is now described as a plan for a coup to take place after the shah's departure from Iran, the writers say that U.S. generals talked with selected Iranian generals about "the long-term possibility that it might be necessary to create a military 'safety net' to prevent the country from falling into total chaos." But the article concludes that "in reality, there was no such safety net, so far as can be discovered." For President Carter, some observers hold, the writers' most damaging accusations may prove to be their contention that the Administration never adopted a clear, consistent policy line—a problem frequently alleged to be at the core of Carter Administration difficulties over other foreign policy issues. The *Washington Quarterly* article says the Carter Administration was internally divided over Iran, with rival factions countermanding each other's orders and eventually paralyzing the U.S. response.

The article asserts that Carter's national security adviser, Zbigniew Brzezinski, wanted disorder repressed with what the shah called "the iron fist." Recommending a different policy, State Department officials led by Secretary of State Cyrus Vance had urged as early as November 1978 that the shah should be persuaded to compromise with a reformist regime such as the Shahpur Bakhtiar government that briefly replaced him, the magazine reports. The article contends that State Department influence was not strong enough to get the United States to open contacts with other Iranian political forces and pave the way for a post-shah Iran but that it hobbled the shah by insisting that he not behave in a way that would antagonize human rights advocates in the United States.

With the bureaucracy at odds, the article continues, "the result was a series of hastily improvised and often self-defeating actions that added impetus to the events in Iran." The shah himself, unable to imagine that a superpower would fumble away a strategic ally such as Iran, remained convinced for weeks after his overthrow that the U.S. government had pursued a grand strategy to manage political change in Iran. But in fact, the article says, the Carter Administration never came to grips with the Iranian situation.

In what appeared to be an attempted partial rebuttal of the article's allegations, U.S. officials disclosed that the Carter Administration made a last-minute attempt to lay the groundwork for a military coup to block the Ayatollah Khomeini's revolution, but that the rapid disintegration of Iran's military forces made the plans unworkable. According to a report by the *New York Times*, citing these senior officials, General Robert Huyser was sent to Iran as the shah's regime crumbled and was ordered to develop contingency plans for a military coup. The *Times* report gave this version of the last-hour events: Initially, General Huyser had been sent to Iran to keep the military forces intact and loyal to the Bakhtiar government and to prevent the officers from seizing power for the shah or themselves. As opposition mounted to the Bakhtiar government, Washington ordered Huyser in late January to prepare a possible coup. In conversations between President Carter and Brzezinski, the general said that such a coup could be staged on short notice.

The purpose was to install a military government that would keep Khomeini and his supporters from dominating Iranian politics. The future of a military regime, or of any succeeding civilian government, was not considered in detail. The possibility of putting these plans into effect was still being explored by the State Department in the last chaotic hours of the Bakhtiar government. When the final assault by the revolutionary forces began on February 10, extensive military desertions in Iran, coupled with policy disagreements in Washington, turned the plans for a coup into "a pipe dream," officials said. Any hopes for a military coup dissolved during the night as the disintegration of the Iranian armed forces became complete.

U.S. Quest for Stability in the Gulf

Iran Provokes Foreign & Domestic Antagonisms

The overthrow of the Pahlevi regime in early 1979 and the establishment of an ideologically radical but politically weak government in its place set in motion a train of events that, from the American and Western point of view, seriously undermined the security of the Persian Gulf and the Arabian peninsula. Iran's repudiation of CENTO and renunciation of the past policy of policing the Gulf swept away the security arrangements for this vital waterway. The strident anti-American rhetoric of the Khomeini government, which assumed an ominous dimension with the seizure of American embassy personnel as hostages, alienated the United States, thereby depriving Iran of an ally. This connection was vital for Iran because only the U.S. could serve as an effective shield against a possible Soviet move into its vulnerable northern provinces; the Iranian military, moreover, remained dependent on the United States for spare parts for the vast amounts of sophisticated equipment it had stocked in its arsenal.

Iran, which had enjoyed basically good relations with the Arab world under the shah, now succeeded in antagonizing many Arab countries, notably its powerful neighbor Iraq. Strident calls by Shi'ite Islamic leaders in Teheran encouraged subversion among Shi'ite minorities in the Persian Gulf states and renewed old claims to Bahrain that the shah had once made and later renounced. The politically conservative, Sunni-led monarchies in the Gulf were deeply offended by the revolutionary slogans of the Shi'ite government in Teheran, which, it was feared, was bent on exporting its revolution. All the Gulf states had important Shi'ite populations who were considered susceptible to developments in Teheran.

Of special significance was the growing tension between Iran and Iraq. The latter had reason to be concerned about the policies of the Teheran authorities. Iraq's substantial Shi'ite population, which had no effective voice in the Baghdad government, might prove amenable to appeals of Teheran radio calling for the overthrow of the Sunni-led government of President Saddam Hussein. Several years earlier, that same government, acting at the request of the shah, had deported the Ayatollah Khomeini from the holy Iraqi city of Najaf to France. The ayatollah had not forgiven President Hussein for that act. The ill will existing between these two Islamic countries gradually worsened and escalated into incidents of border warfare. Iran accused Baghdad of fomenting unrest among its Kurdish population and encouraging separatist tendencies among the Arab population in its rich oil-producing province of Khuzistan.

Iran also went out of its way to antagonize President Anwar al-Sadat of Egypt for having concluded a peace agreement with Israel. Iran, which rallied behind the Palestine Liberation Organization and declared Israel to be a mortal enemy, accused the Egyptian ruler of selling out the Palestine cause. President Sadat, for his part, indicated unhappiness over the turn of events in Iran that led to the overthrow of the shah. The Iranian monarch had provided

Sadat with vital material support in 1975 when his government faced a severe financial crisis. The ayatollah's Islamic fundamentalist policies provided little basis for accord with Sadat's moderate approach in dealing with his clerics. Along strategic lines, the Egyptian leader obviously feared that Iran's policies would facilitate Soviet encroachment into the Persian Gulf and Arabian peninsula and thereby pose a threat to the Red Sea area, where Moscow had already developed a position of strength in Southern Yemen and Ethiopia.

As if the idiosyncratic behavior of the Khomeini government in foreign affairs was not enough, it added to its troubles by pursuing a repressive policy towards its non-Persian peoples, who comprise about one-third of the country's population. Not unlike the shah, the revolutionary government refused to accede to the demands of these ethnic groups for meaningful autonomy in their internal affairs. Thus, the revolutionary Iranian leadership which came to power ostensibly for the reason of putting an end to the tyranny of the shah, became embroiled in one conflict after another with Iran's Kurdish, Baluchi, Arab and other ethnic minorities. These were peoples who had initially supported the Khomeini-led revolution against the shah in the expectation that it would lead to a democratic Iran.

What the ethnic minorities had hoped for was the establishment of a decentralized form of government in which important powers would be delegated to the provinces. Under such decentralized rule, the ethnic populations assumed that they would have direct responsibility for such governmental functions as education, agriculture and local taxation. As it turned out, these expectations did not materialize. The new constitution called for the establishment of a highly centralized government in which virtually all important functions were administered by the authorities in Teheran. This new, Islamic-inspired constitution served as a red flag to the non-Persian populations, which felt cheated of their fruits of the revolution. Not surprisingly, a substantial measure of the government's energies was devoted to suppressing uprisings of these groups against its authority. In these bloody encounters, the government employed tanks, helicopter gunships and artillery to enforce its authority.

What further exacerbated relations between many of the ethnic populations and the central government were religious differences. Foremost among these was the inclusion of a provision in the new constitution making Shi'ite Islam the official religion of Iran. Many of the ethnic groups, notably the Kurds, Turkomen, Baluchis and Arabs, professed the Sunni form of Islam. Given the importance of religion in the politics of the revolutionary state, this aspect of the constitution could not but help alienate even more the non-Persian peoples. Compounding their differences with the central authorities over the issue of national rights, these groups had to accept a constitution in which Sunni Islam did not enjoy the same measure of protection under the constitution as the dominant Shi'a form.

It was against these ethnic and religious differences that widespread rebellion broke out in Kurdistan, Baluchistan, Khuzistan and other parts of the country. In the important oil-producing province of Khuzistan, sixty per cent of whose population is Arab, there has been a growing incidence of sabotage of oil installations and attacks on government officials. In one major outbreak of guerrilla activity in the fall of 1980, the government summarily executed eleven suspected Arab conspirators. And in the Kurdish regions, important elements of the weakened Iranian army, along with Revolutionary Guards, were tied down by Kurdish insurgents determined to win their demands against the government.

While Iran went about creating new enemies and alienating old friends, the revolutionary government began to reduce the armed forces to a shadow of what they had been under the shah. Many ranking officers were executed, imprisoned or cashiered, and much of the sophisticated equipment that the shah had acquired at great expense was rendered useless for lack of spare parts and proper maintenance. After the seizure of the American hostages, President Carter embargoed the sale of all goods to Iran. The effect of this was to demoralize the once-powerful military establishment and reduce its effectiveness in safeguarding the nation against internal insurrection and possible external attacks. Ironically, the revolutionary authorities, in their zeal to purge the military, which was the only organized group in the country that had the means to overthrow the government, and reasons enough for doing so, made the country into a tempting target for the revolution's enemies.

Instability in the Yemens

Although developments in post-shah Iran constituted the main threat to stability in the Persian Gulf, other sources of tension emerged that posed serious problems as well. Only weeks after the shah's downfall, Marxist Southern Yemen (the People's Democratic Republic of Yemen) provoked open clashes with the politically moderate (Northern) Yemen (the Yemen Arab Republic), a state having close ties to Saudi Arabia. To some, the fighting seemed a continuation of the on-again, off-again warfare between the two Yemens. However, coming hard on the heels of the revolution in Iran, Saudi Arabia indicated fear that this latest outbreak in hostilities could usher in a new era of political instability in its backyard. In the summer of 1978 both Yemens had been embroiled in political violence that claimed the lives of the rulers of the two countries. The first act of violence, whose exact details still remain shrouded in mystery, occurred in June with the assassination of North Yemen's President Ahmed Hussein al-Ghashmi by means of a bomb planted in the briefcase of an envoy from President Salem Robaye Ali of Southern Yemen. The murder was first blamed on Robaye Ali and was cited as a factor in his overthrow and execution two days later by colleagues in

Southern Yemen's pro-Soviet National Front. But the main Northern Yemeni newspaper, *Al Thawra*, suggested that President Ali had been absolved of culpability for President Ghashmi's death. *Al Thawra* reported that Northern Yemeni authorities believed the envoy's briefcase was switched on the private plane that flew him from Aden to Sana, the capital of Northern Yemen. It said the original briefcase was believed to have contained a genuine message from Robaye Ali to Ghashmi asking him for clemency for Yemenis who had recently defected to Aden, Southern Yemen's capital.

President Robaye Ali's execution left Southern Yemen even more closely allied with the Soviet Union. Though a leftist like the rest of the governing National Liberation Front's leadership, he was said to have maintained secret contacts with the conservative government of neighboring Saudi Arabia, and *Al Safir*, a leftist, Beirut-based newspaper, reported that other Front leaders who ordered his execution had discovered these contacts. Robaye Ali's elimination put Southern Yemen's leadership into the hands of a troika headed by Abdul Fattah Ismail, a pro-Soviet Marxist ideologue. The Soviet Union, which has a naval base at Aden, emerged as a direct beneficiary of the power struggle in this arid, impoverished state, whose strategic location could give the Soviets potential control of vital oil routes through the Red Sea and Suez Canal.

The mini-warfare between the Yemens rekindled Saudi fears of communist "encirclement" and of regional unrest. The Saudis were particularly jittery over this crisis, the first in the region since the overthrow of the shah, because they tended to assume that it was Soviet inspired. The Southern Yemenis were regarded as unlikely to have acted without the tacit consent of their Soviet ally. Many observers in the region shared the view that Moscow, eager to capitalize on America's acute discomfiture in the Persian Gulf, was about to open a new front by promoting a proxy war in the Arabian peninsula. This was seen by many Arab analysts as the first visible fallout of the turmoil in Iran. It was a source of deep concern to the Saudis for strategic reasons. They feared that the better-disciplined and Soviet-equipped Southern Yemeni army might succeed in unseating North-ern Yemen's rulers and uniting the two Yemens as a single Marxist state. A unified Yemen, far larger in population than Saudi Arabia, would pose a serious threat to the oil-rich kingdom. It would permit the Kremlin to exercise a virtually unchallenged position of strength in the peninsula. Under such circumstances, the Saudis might have no other choice than to become more amenable to sharing their oil with the Soviet Union in the 1980s, when Moscow for the first time is expected to be shopping the world over for crude oil.

The war also had disturbing regional overtones for the Saudis. Northern Yemen has been important as a source of labor—a half million Yemenis work in the kingdom—and as a buffer to the Soviet presence in the Horn of Africa. For some time, Southern Yemen, the Arab world's only declared Marxist state, had been smuggling infiltrators and weapons across the border into Northern Yemen. In the Sultanate of Oman to the east, Aden has for years abetted a leftist guer-rilla war. In 1975, Iranian forces finally quelled the rebellion in Oman's Dhofar province. Now, with these troops having been recalled by Khomeini, there had concern in Oman and Saudi Arabia about the revival of the insurgency.

Clearly alarmed by the undeclared war on its southern border, Riyadh announced February 28, 1979 a cancellation of all military leaves in its 60,000-man army and declared a state of partial mobilization. It also prepared to bring home its 1,200-man peacekeeping continegent in Lebanon, part of an all-Arab force that had been assembled to restore peace in this war-ravaged country. These moves coincided with intensive diplomatic efforts by the Saudis and the Arab League to bring about an end to the conflict. In 1972, an Arab League mediation commission had succeeded in work-ing out a cease-fire in a border war between the hostile countries.

While these regional efforts at peacemaking were developing, intensive consultations were taking place between Washington and Riyadh. The nervous Saudi government was anxious to end the conflict in concert with its U.S. ally. In early March of 1979 reports circulated that Saudi Arabia had sought American support for a possible Saudi intervention on the side of North Yemen. The Saudis had asked for permission, as required under American law, to use American-built weapons in the action against Southern Yemen. The Carter Administration quickly responded by offering to send a squadron of Air Force fighters to Saudi Arabia, a move that was intended to facilitate possible Saudi involvement in the fighting. Under the U.S. offer, the American squadron, 18 armed F-15s, would be used to protect the country while the Saudi Air Force helped North Yemen in its effort to repel the Soviet-supplied forces of South Yemen. As it developed, the Saudis declined Washington's offer because it was wary about too close an identification with the United States. A principal reason for this official reticence was Saudi unhappiness over Washington's role in promoting the Egyptian-Israeli peace agreement, an accord that the Saudis and most Arab countr.es felt ignored the Palestine question.

Washington had readied other measures to deal with this emerging threat to the stability of the Arabian peninsula and to the security of Saudi Arabia. On March 8, President Carter approved a military aid plan for Northern Yemen that called for the immediate delivery of $390 million worth of armaments, including 12 P-5 fighter planes, tanks and personnel carriers. Administration officials said that the arms would be shipped first to Saudi Arabia, which would pay for them, and that they would be assembled there and made ready for combat by Saudi and American military technicians. The Pentagon said that fewer than 100 Americans would be sent to Yemen and that none would be involved in combat missions. The President signed a waiver to permit the delivery of the weapons without the normal thirty-day Congressional review period. Under the 1976 Arms Export Control Act, this Congressional review requirement can be waived by the President if he determines that national security interests warrant speedy delivery.

Shaping a New U.S. Security Policy for the Region

The immediate aim of the Carter Administration was to bring about an end to hostilities between the two Yemens. This did indeed occur although it came about through a combination of Arab-sponsored diplomatic activity as well as the powerful American reponse. The truce between the two Yemens was strongly urged on Southern Yemen by Syria and Iraq, working in tandemn with Saudi Arabia and the Persian Gulf states. The Soviets, who had used Cubans, East Germans and Ethiopians in Southern Yemen's war against Northern Yemen, had an agonizing choice once the Iraqis, Syrians and Saudis joined forces to stop the border warfare. That choice was either to alienate Saudi Arabia (which had been making faint overtures to Moscow as a result of the changing world balance of power) and the Soviet friends Syria and Iraq by continuing the war, or to antagonize the pro-Soviet Marxists in its client state of Southern Yemen by urging that the border war be ended. The realists in the Kremlin did not take long in making their choice. The war came to a sudden halt by March 17, 1979, and the American military supplies piled up in Sana's airport without having been put to use beyond training.

The White House, noting the conclusion of a cease-fire, argued that the Administration's strong response already had paid off. It is difficult to assess this judgement in light of the efforts of an Arab League team, after visits to Northern and Southern Yemen, in arranging the cease-fire. Depsite the end of hostilities, Washington went ahead with its commitment to send the nearly $400 million worth of military aid along with a small number of military technicians. Washington and Riyadh were anxious to strengthen Northern Yemen to deter further attacks from its neighbor to the south. Northern Yemen was seen as essential to protect access to the Red Sea through the Bab al Mandab Strait, which Southern Yemen already partially controls from its capital, Aden, and from strong points on Perim Island and Socotra Island. Soviet naval ships and aircraft have operated out of Aden for some time. Communist-bloc advisers were reported to have arrived in considerable strength at the time of the fighting. The conservative Kuwaiti newspaper *Al Siyasa* reported that the Soviet Union and Cuba had rushed troops and advisers to Southern Yemen. The newspaper placed the number at nearly 3,000 Cuban soldiers and Soviet military advisers, who had been sent to South Yemen around the first week of March. Administration officials estimated that there were about 800 Soviet advisers in the country, 300 to 500 Cuban advisers and about 100 East Germans.

President Carter's decision to send military aid and advisers to Northern Yemen was only marginally related to the presence of Soviet and East bloc military advisers in Southern Yemen. They and been there for some time. Rather, the President acted to demonstrate to domestic critics and to friendly countries in the region, particularly Saudi Arabia, that the United States was prepared to protect American interests in the oil-producing region. There was a strong need to rebuild Washington's credibility among moderate governments in the region. Until these actions, Carter had avoided shows of force in dealing with the Gulf region. In December 1978 he had decided not to send the aircraft carrier *Constellation* into the Indian Ocean as a symbol of American support for the ill-fated government appointed by the shah. Similarly, a year earlier, Carter had refused to let America become involved in the border war between Ethiopia and Somalia across the Red Sea and Gulf of Aden from the Yemens, even though there was pressure on him to intervene on behalf of Somalia. This time, according to White House aides, one of the strongest proponents of a military response over Yemen had been the President.

The President's actions in this flare-up of fighting in the Arabian peninsula should, in a more fundamental sense, be understood within the context of America's strategic interests in the entire Persian Gulf-Arabian peninsula and Red Sea region. Since the collapse of the shah, Washington had become acutely aware of the need to evolve a new strategic concept for the defense of this oil-rich, strategic region. The shah's armed forces were no longer available to protect the region; and Saudi Arabia's limited military power was an inadequate substitute for this formidable task. While a strong response was designed to allay Saudi fears, it was also intended to serve as a basis for a possible new approach for safeguarding the Gulf area.

This new approach had been alluded to earlier by both the Secretary of Defense and the Secretary of Energy, who warned that the United States would defend its vital interests in the Middle East and Persian Gulf with military force if necessary.

Harold Brown, the Defense Secretary, said: "The United States is prepared to defend its vital interests with whatever means are appropriate, including military force where necessary, whether that's in the Middle East or elsewhere." Appearing on the CBS News program "Face the Nation," Brown said that protection of the oil flow from the Middle East "is clearly part of our vital interest." "I said," he continued, "and I repeat, that in the protection of those vital interests we'll take any action that's appropriate, including the use of military force. But military force is not necessarily appropriate in every individual instance." Asked for specifics, Brown demurred: "The only thing I would say is that less intrusive and less obvious forms of U.S. presence or possibly military influence, such as ship visits and so on, are clearly the right way to begin such activities, and I think that may be as far as we want to go."

In a separate interview, James R. Schlesinger, Secretary of Energy, said the Carter Administration was considering a plan to establish an American military presence in the Persian Gulf region. "The United States," he asserted, "has vital

interests in the Persian Gulf. The United States must move
in such a way that it protects those interests, even if that
involves the use of military strength, of military presence."
Asked about sending troops, the former CIA Director and
Defense Secretary, said: "I think that will have to be considered, quite plainly. If we are considering a military presence, that would involve military personnel as well as
equipment." But he said that sending ground combat troops
"is another question."

It is against the background of these statements by these
two senior Cabinet officials that one should understand the
larger strategic role that Washington was developing for the
defense of the region. In January 1979, after the Administration decided not to despatch the *Constellation* into the
Indian Ocean in support of the shah, it did agree to respond
to an appeal from Saudi Arabia for a show of force in the
region. The United States sent a dozen F-15s, which, it was
later learned, were unarmed, and 300 members of the Air
Force, to that nation in a demonstration of American support. The actions of the President in the Yemeni crisis, and
the decision to send the squadron of F-15s to Saudi Arabia,
were part of the new Administration strategy for the defense
of the region. In now ordering the *Constellation* into the
Arabian Sea, the President meant not only to impress Saudi
Arabia, but to demonstrate to President Anwar el-Sadat of
Egypt that the United States was prepared to back up its
friends. Thus, showing the flag in Yemen was described as a
first step in an unfolding strategy of compensating for the
loss of Iran by stitching together a loose alliance of moderate
Arab nations that, together with Israel and increased American naval and air power, could serve as a bulwark against
regional instability and Soviet penetration. "You've got to
understand," said one White House aide, "that our actions
in Yemen and the Middle East peace process are intimately
linked. Both form part of a wider policy of salvaging American influence in the area after Iran."

The Administration policy in Yemen was not without its
critics. At a hearing before a House Foreign Affairs subcom-

mittee, Administration spokesmen were peppered with angry questions by Democrats. Representative Lee Hamilton of Indiana, the subcommittee chairman, demanded to know why it was necessary for the President to invoke emergency powers in rushing arms to Yemen. Representative Gerry Studds of Massachusetts charged that in sending warplanes and tanks, the Administration was ignoring the lessons of the revolution in Iran. And in a separate statement, Representative Les Aspin of Wisconsin compared Carter's quick decisions to send military advisers to Yemen with the early phases of American involvement in Vietnam. "We are building up Yemen for, at the very least, a strong American role in a Saudi military campaign against South Yemen, and possibly for a direct American role—all without a great deal of thought," he said. Aspen stated that U.S. arms deliveries to Northern Yemen in 1979 would total $540 million, making it the largest recipient of American weapons after Israel and Saudi Arabia. He charged that "We are delivering $540 million in sophisticated weaponry to an army with fewer than 1,000 soldiers who can read or write." In a speech prepared for delivery to Congress March 13, Congressman Aspen charged that the Administration's measures seemed to be based on the idea of "jumping in because it's the first thing to come along since the decision to change our foreign policy." "Yemen may be a particularly bad bet on which to wager our prestige. North and South Yemen are divided by age-old tribal wars.... Tribes shift alliances regularly, often depending on which side is offering the more attractive bribe," he added. The Congressman also cited reports that the Northern Yemeni army was not even fighting against Southern Yemen, "because the tribal members who are acting as mercenaries for the Saudis get higher wages."

Stronger U.S. Policy in the Region

A U.S. aircraft carrier steaming toward the Arabian Sea; American radar planes patrolling the skies of Saudi Arabia;

U.S. military advisers and arms going to a brush-war in faroff Yemen—all these measures represented an unexpected military response to the conflict and ushered in a new phase of American foreign policy. President Carter's decision to flex American military muscle in support of Northern Yemen against Soviet-backed Southern Yemen was partially obscured by the high drama of the Middle East peace process. This U.S.-directed production resulted in the conclusion of a treaty ending the generation-old war between Egypt and Israel. Yet few officials quarreled with the argument that the Carter Administration's decision to aid Northern Yemen and its oil-rich benefactor, Saudi Arabia, could have a favorable impact on stability in the Middle East and the Persian Gulf. This more muscular policy, which would hardly have seemed conceivable a few months earlier, met with general public approval. Even potential Republican contenders for the presidency, such as Senator Howard Baker, praised Carter for, as they put it, finally shedding his inhibitions about exercising American military power.

Underlying this new approach was a perceived need for the United States to bring far greater military power to bear than it already had within the region. One such measure was to augment the American fleet operating in the Indian Ocean. A policy option under consideration was to create a new naval force, to be called the Fifth Fleet, which would bolster American military might in the region. The Soviet invasion of Afghanistan accelerated the movement in Washington to shore up American influence in the area through greater reliance on military power. For many Western observers, the defense of Western oil supplies in the Persian Gulf from local turmoil and possible Soviet military threats had become equal in importance to the American commitment to Western Europe and Japan.

Under the impact of Iran and Afghanistan, the Carter Administration had been forced to abandon many of the foreign policy goals it had unveiled on coming to office in 1977. Earlier objectives of promoting human rights, restraining arms exports and curbing the spread of nuclear technology were now overshadowed by more traditional security concerns. As noted in an earlier chapter, the most obvious changes had taken place in policy toward the Soviet Union and in the past commitment to dampening East-West military competition. The Administration had earlier pledged never to use food as a weapon and had declined to link Soviet actions in Third World countries to progress in arms control. It reacted to Moscow's intervention in Afghanistan, however, by cancelling grain shipments to the Soviets and postponing the Senate debate on the SALT II nuclear arms treaty.

The enunciation by President Carter of his policy to defend the Persian Gulf, by military force if necessary, represented a fundamental shift, not in Carter policy but in positions adopted by previous administrations. Actually, as Stanley Hoffman, professor of government at Harvard University, wrote, the Carter position was "not so much a new foreign policy as a repudiation of two familiar notions of the 1970s." One is the Nixon Doctrine, Hoffman wrote, and the other the assumption that U.S. relations with the Soviet Union could be "treated as a less important issue than, and a separate problem from, the global issues of world order such as human rights, nonproliferation and energy. The Carter message, on the contrary, stresses the interaction between Soviet conduct and these issues. . . . " In regard to the Nixon Doctrine, Hoffman observed: "We have discovered that we cannot rely on other nations to meet major Soviet challenges with limited assistance from us and that there is no substitute for our own forces."*

President Carter's decision to send arms to Yemen in early 1979 and the despatch of F-15 planes to Saudi Arabia already suggested that the United States was moving away from relying upon other nations for the defense of its inter-

---

*Stanley Hoffman, "Toward A Foreign Policy," *New York Times*, Op. Ed. January 25, 1980.

ests in the Persian Gulf. It had expressed willingness to send
support planes to Saudi Arabia in the event the latter
became involved in the Yemeni war. This involvement did
not materialize, in part because the war did not last long but
more fundamentally owing to the reluctance of the Saudis to
become too closely indentified with the United States.
Washington's support of the peace process chilled relations
with the Saudis, a not unexpected development in view of
the considerable influence exercised by the Palestine Liberation Organization in Saudi Arabia and the Gulf states.
Because of the large numbers of Palestinians in these countries,* many of whom work in the oil fields, their governments fear the possibility of sabotage of the oil installations.
PLO influence in the region grew even more following the
coming to power in Iran of the Ayatollah Khomeini, a
staunch supporter of the Palestinian cause.

Despite Saudi reluctance to become too visibly associated
with the United States, and, it should be noted, indecision
within the Carter Administration over how far it should go
in the use of military power to deal with problems in the
region, Washington was becoming increasingly committed
to the principle of using its own military power to safeguard
its interests in the Gulf. What increasingly concerned the
Administration was the magnitude of the military forces
required to discharge the new commitment and the readi-
ness of the countries around the Persian Gulf to join in the
new policy. The biggest question concerned the circumstances, besides a Soviet invasion of Iran or other oil-
producing nations, that might lead President Carter to order
military forces into the Persian Gulf.

These questions had been the focus of debate among
Carter Administration officials for more than a year. In

---

*About 250,000 Palestinians make up nearly a quarter of the population
of Kuwait; another 50,000 work in Saudi Arabia, and roughly 50,000 live
in other states on the Arabian peninsula. "There is a silent tension
between the Palestinians and those states," it is widely agreed, because
their governments fear they might do harm to the national interest.

mid-1977, Zbigniew Brzezinski, Carter's national security adviser, took a step toward extending a security umbrella over the Persian Gulf by advocating the creation of a rapid deployment force for use in Third World crises. Responding to this advice, Carter issued a directive in August 1977 calling for the establishment of such a force. There was opposition to the plan in the Pentagon, where there was concern that it would divert resources from Western Europe, and in the State Department, where it was felt that the intervention unit would be politically provocative. As a result, little had been done during 1978 to bring such a force into being. Instead, the Administration adhered to the Persian Gulf strategy favored during the Nixon and Ford administrations, relying on Iran to protect Western interests and providing the shah with modern weapons.

This policy, however, collapsed with the the overthrow of the shah a year later. The Iranian revolution raised serious questions in other states in the region about United States reliability and marked a turning point in American strategy. In late February 1979, Brzezinski pressed the President to approve an increase in the U.S. military role in the area, including arms sales, a naval presence in the Indian Ocean and the possible establishment of military bases. The problems of playing a more assertive role in the region were underscored when Secretary of Defense Harold Brown visited Saudi Arabia and other countries to discuss military cooperation. He found several countries eager to receive arms but generally cool to the idea of having American troops on their soil.

These findings led the Administration to defer looking for possible bases and, in meetings through the spring of 1979, senior aides focused on the presence of American naval forces in nearby parts of the Indian Ocean. In June, Warren M. Christopher, the Deputy Secretary of State, and Harold H. Saunders, the Assistant Secretary for Near Eastern and South Asian Affairs, were said to have argued that any attempt to increase American naval forces would prompt a

corresponding Soviet naval buildup. Brzezinski, together
with Defense Secretary Brown and Energy Secretary James
R. Schlesinger, reportedly prevailed in inducing the President to accept the notion that the United States should be
the preponderant naval power. Accordingly, Carter approved a plan for increased visits by aircraft carrier task
forces in the Indian Ocean.

Three months later, during dispute over the presence of a
Soviet combat brigade in Cuba, Brzezinski was able to gain
Carter's support in pushing the Pentagon to accelerate plans
for the rapid deployment force. But while the Administration was gradually moving to augment its capacity to intervene, the twin crises in Iran and Afghanistan made a new
policy inevitable. In the case of Iran, White House aides
were said to have been shocked by how few military options
the United States had at its disposal. The Soviet move into
Afghanistan led the President to revise his estimate of Soviet
intentions. While the situation in Afghanistan forced the
Administration to consider the possibility of further Soviet
thrusts into Iran or Pakistan, few officials seemed to believe
that this was the most likely source of instability. They said
they expected Moscow to attempt to take advantage of
internal disruptions and regional conflicts by expanding its
influence in indirect ways.

Well before President Carter set forth his doctrine for the
defense of the Persian Gulf, the United States revealed a
disposition to use military and other means for protecting its
interests in the Middle East and the Gulf. As part of the
peace agreement signed by Egypt and Israel March 26, 1979,
the Carter Administration committed the United States to a
direct role in monitoring its implementation. Regular reconnaissance flights by high-flying U-2 aircraft from the British
base at Akrotiri, Cyprus were to observe compliance with
the agreement. The United States had, as part of the second
Egyptian-Israeli disengagement agreement of 1975, agreed
to maintain monitoring posts near the Mitla and Giddi

passes. Unofficially, U.S. naval forces acted in a back-up capacity for the Saudi navy for the safeguarding of the Straits of Hormuz following the overthrow of the shah. With the PLO solidly entrenched in revolutionary Iran, the danger of subversion by radical Palestinian elements to the oil fields and oil supply lanes along the Arab-ruled east coast of the Gulf had increased. Ever since a Palestinian speed-boat had tried to sink an Israel-bound tanker, the *Coral Sea*, in the Red Sea straits off Yemen in 1968, Western defense planners have worried about the possible sinking or sabotage of a tanker, thus blocking the straits and stopping the oil flow to the West and Far East.

Another area of growing U.S. military concern was the Indian Ocean. In 1977, both the United States and the Soviet Union committed themselves to the demilitarization of the Indian Ocean. As long as the United States was able to insure access to Gulf oil, there was no substantial need to maintain a naval presence in the ocean. With growing instability in the Gulf region and given the Soviet invasion of Afghanistan, U.S. military planners shelved plans for demilitarizing the Indian Ocean. Actually, the Soviets had become increasingly suspicious of U.S. aims in the Indian Ocean, accusing Washington of expanding its military presence there by building a base on the island of Diego Garcia. Moscow had contended that the presence of a Soviet fleet in the area did not contradict its call for the Indian Ocean to become a "zone of peace."

Subsequent to the withdrawal of the British east of Suez in 1971, several factors have made the Indian Ocean region increasingly a flash point in great-power maneuvering. Among these considerations:

•The crude oil shipping lanes have become an "increasingly swollen jugular" out of the Persian Gulf into the Indian Ocean west to European ports and east to Japan—regions of the world that depend almost exclusively on Arab and Iranian oil imports.

•The Suez Canal has become less of a factor in shipping Persian Gulf crude as a result of the 1967-75 closure and the advent of supertankers that are too large to transit the canal.

•The Soviet Union, which has legitimate interests in the area, has for many years been concerned about the possibility of war with China. The Soviet general staff understands that in the event of a war, a Chinese thrust against the Trans-Siberian Railway could cut off the Soviet Far East from central Russia, leaving the Indian Ocean as the main route for ship-borne supplies from the Black Sea to Vladivostock.

•Growing demands for protein have cast a new spotlight on the Indian Ocean. As more and more nations nail up "no fishing" signs at their 200-mile limits, international waters that contain or are suspected to contain rich supplies of fish become potential targets of influence jobbing. Two of the most important untapped sources of fish are in the Indian Ocean and the South Atlantic.

In a period of true detente, the superpowers might have succeeded in concluding an agreement for the demilitarization of the Indian Ocean, or failing that, placing limits on the deployment of warships there. That became progressively more difficult as Soviet political ambitions developed in Somalia, Ethiopia and in the Sudan. Ethiopia, having turned away from a long period of friendship with the United States, had embraced the Soviets, who were now well positioned along the Red Sea. And if the United States had a "crescent of crisis," the Soviets seemed to be suffering from one too. The Soviets were genuinely concerned at the prospect of the United States underwriting the Egyptian-Israeli peace agreement—and at other U.S. regional actions, such as moving the aircraft carrier *Constellation*, sending arms and advisers to Yemen and openly discussing the creation of a "Fifth Fleet" based in the Indian Ocean. There also was expressed Soviet concern over the United States' naval facilities on Diego Garcia in the Chagos Archipelago south of India. Kremlin comments on developments in Iran and

Afghanistan indicated Soviet problems there, too. Growing opposition to the Khomeini government in Iran and to the Marxist regime in Afghanistan created situations of growing chaos in two countries bordering on the Soviet Union. Historically, Moscow has been ultra-sensitive to conditions in bordering states that could, directly, or indirectly, influence political developments inside the Soviet Union. Given the latter's large Muslim population in its central Asian republics, numbering about 50 million people, there was a possibility that elements of this population could be influenced by the Islamic revolution that was sweeping Iran and that, in part, inspired the Afghan tribesmen to take up arms against Soviet invaders.

The Soviets, not surprisingly, increased their naval and air activity in the Indian Ocean and adjacent land areas. While the U.S. Navy was trying to scrape together a small squadron (the projected Fifth Fleet) for service in the Indian Ocean, the Soviet Union maintained 18 to 20 ships in those waters. This was in addition to important naval elements that Moscow had despatched from its Pacific Fleet into the South China Sea to demonstrate its support for Vietnam during the border war with China at the beginning of 1979. These naval deployments underscored the point made by Admiral Sergei G. Gorshkov that the Soviet navy had achieved "significantly greater operational capabilities." Reflecting on the comment made by Gorshkov, who is the commander of the Soviet navy, Rear Admiral Sumner Shapiro, director of U.S. Naval Intelligence, said there was every indication that the Russians intended to use their navy to extend "Soviet military, political and economic influence throughout the world." Improvements in the number and quality of Soviet warships, according to Admiral Shapiro, would allow the Soviet navy to provide Moscow with "political and military options heretofore unavailable."

Among the concerns of U.S. naval strategists is that the Soviet fleet has been rapidly losing dependence on shore bases. During the early spring maneuvers in the Mediterranean in 1979, the new Soviet aircraft carriers *Minsk* and *Kiev* operated together with surface ships for the first time. The big Soviet supply ship *Berezina* was able to refuel three ships at once. The Soviet navy has been deploying near Western oil supply lines from the Persian Gulf and in waters on the northern flank of Europe, where NATO perceives a growing threat. Since March 14, 1979, as part of its spring maneuvers, the two Soviet carrier groups, including missile ships, both nuclear and conventional submarines, and aircraft, have fanned out from the Black Sea and Mediterranean for exercises in three ocean areas. After the Mediterranean exercises north of Libya, the *Minsk* group sailed from Gibraltar through the South Atlantic around Africa, calling at Mauritius in the Indian Ocean. Its vessels later operated near Western oil tanker lanes at Socotra Island, in the Arabian Sea. Land-based Soviet reconnaissance and bombing planes from Aden, in nearby South Yemen, supported the *Minsk* and its helicopters and vertical takeoff planes.

In response to the continuing tension with Iran over the hostage issue, and probably to counter the Soviet naval buildup, President Carter despatched in November 1979 a second naval task force, including the aircraft carrier *Kitty Hawk*, into the Indian Ocean south of Iran. The ships, sent from the U.S. base at Subic Bay in the Philippines, required a week to ten days to reach the Arabian Sea, where they could take up position. The movement of these ships to the Indian Ocean was intended as a show of military force to the Teheran government.

U.S. Strength Policy & Search for Bases in the Region

If the Soviet Union needed evidence that it had touched a raw American nerve with its invasion of Afghanistan, it came in the thunderclap of applause in Congress to President Carter's State of the Union speech in 1980 warning that he was ready to use force to protect vital American interests in the Persian Gulf.

Reflecting the public mood, Capital Hill was caught up in a wave of nationalistic fervor, angered, anxious, frustrated and feisty, above all determined to react to the Soviet actions. The mood was not as belligerent as the crisis atmosphere that had swept aside all objections in August 1964, when an earlier Congress passed the Gulf of Tonkin Resolution and prepared the way for American expeditionary forces to intervene in Vietnam. But so strong was the urge in this new post-Afghan period to punish the Russians that only a few voices of dissent rose when the Congress overwhelmingly voted to support the President's plan to boycott the Moscow Olympic Games. There was a bandwagon sentiment after Carter ticked off his proposals for a rapid deployment force, higher defense spending, less restraint on intelligence activities, aid to Pakistan, an American presence and access to military facilities around the fringes of the Indian Ocean, and for reviving draft registration in peacetime. "Even the most rational and cautious members are going to ride this bandwagon no matter what their doubts about particular spending proposals," said Senator Edmund Muskie. "I wish and I hope that we'll do all this in as rational a way as possible. But there's a risk we'll overreact. Nothing so stimulates the spending instinct in Congress as a threat to our national security."

The crises in Iran and in Afghanistan brought about an important shift of attitudes in the American public that, in the view of some analysts, is likely to have a significant impact on the willingness of the United States to project its power in the Third World and to develop greater capabilities for protecting its interests there. The Iranian situation, involving a threat to Western oil interests, and the humiliation over the seizure of the hostages, served to galvanize public sentiment in support of a more activist type of foreign policy. George W. Ball, a former Under Secretary of State, captured the sense of many in Washington when he said, a month before the Soviet invasion of Afghanistan, that the nation was overcoming "it sense of guilt, its complexes over the Vietnam War." A number of politicians and officials held that the trend had long been in the making. "Its not just Iran," said Senator Gary Hart, Democrat of Colorado. "We have been through a period of shocks over the past five years since the fall of Saigon, the formation of OPEC and the oil embargo. There's increased nationalism abroad, less fear of the United States—not because we're less potent but because others are more potent." This shift in public sentiment also reflects a reported fear on the part of many Americans that the Soviet Union has gained military superiority over the United States. Ben J. Wattenberg, chairman of the Coalition for a Democratic Majority and a senior fellow at the American Enterprise Insititute, a conservative "think tank," wrote in the *New York Times Magazine* that the crux of the new mood in Washington can be defined as "the dawn of old ideas in a new era." He asserted that "the old chestnut of 'peace through strength' makes ever greater sense." This more militant public mood expressed itself in greater support for defense spending and a willingness to intervene abroad in the event of a military crisis. At the time of the Yemen crisis, there was little public criticism of Carter's decision to send arms and military advisers to that country.

Despite greater willingness to support a more muscular type of foreign policy, the United States' capacity to intervene in such areas as the Persian Gulf and Arabian peninsula was greatly circumscribed. America's political reach, it was generally acknowledged, exceeded its military grasp. If America's new Persian Gulf policy was to have credibility in the Kremlin and among America's Third World allies, there had to be an increase in available military power in these regions. And for the United States to be able to project its military strength in these areas on a sustained basis, it had to have at its disposal military bases or, at a minimum, access to military facilities.

The Iranian crisis, which underscored the strategic importance of the Persian Gulf, accelerated Administration plans for creating a 110,000-man "rapid-deployment force" for use in military conflicts in the area. Although such a force had the strong backing of Defense Secretary Brown and of national security adviser Brzezinski, the proposal has, since it was proposed in 1977, generated controversy in the Administration because it could presage a new phase of military involvement in the Indian Ocean and Persian Gulf. The creation of the force would also represent a significant departure from the Administration's overall military strategy, which had concentrated on shoring up American forces in Western Europe at the expense of strength for intervening in the Third World. The Iranian crisis, as well as the dispute with Moscow over Soviet troops in Cuba, had given new impetus to the Pentagon's plan. Brzezinski had favored the establishment of the force in 1977; and a hardliner toward the Kremlin, he had helped persuade the President of the need for a rapid-deployment force.

The United States has had the ability to intervene in military conflicts around the globe since World War II. The Marine Corps, 180,000 men strong, is equipped and trained for fighting in small "brush-fire" wars. A large fraction of the Army's 82nd Airborne Division has been placed on continuous alert and, according to defense officials, could be flown anywhere in the world within twenty-four hours. Under current plans, the rapid deployment force would be drawn from existing Marine and Army troops stationed in the United States. In the event of a major conflict, existing C-5A transport planes and a new long-range aircraft, known as the CX, would ferry troops to the region of conflict. The Navy would keep a fleet of cargo ships in the Indian Ocean, stocked with military equipment.

Proponents of the rapid-deployment force contend, as President Carter argued in a speech in early October 1979, that "we must be able to move our ground, sea and air units to distant areas—rapidly and with adequate supplies." While acknowledging that the United States could intervene in foreign conflicts, many defense officials have long contended that existing interventionary forces are too slow and too small. Brzezinski, for example, had been known to hold that the outcome of any Soviet-American military confrontation in the Persian Gulf would be determined by the speed with which the two sides could send forces to the area. Beyond the military arguments, the Administration and many outside observers, such as former Secretary of State Henry A. Kissinger, had maintained that the creation of a special interventionary force would demonstrate the Administration's commitment to maintaining political stability in the Gulf.

Opponents of the force proposal contended that it was unnecessary and politically provocative. Some critics of the plan contended that a large interventionary force would be of little use in crises, such as the Iranian revolution, that stemmed mainly from internal unrest. Military forces, it also had been argued, could not block Soviet political penetration in the Persian Gulf. As for the threat of Soviet military intervention, some State Department officals maintained that Moscow would be unwilling to threaten Western oil interests for fear of touching off a full-scale Soviet-American war. Other critics of the concept have contended that Persian Gulf oil could not be defended by military means. Richard J. Barnet, a senior fellow of the Washington-based Institute for Policy Studies and a frequent critic of the Pentagon, said that while the U.S. could intervene in the region, it would be unable in the long-run to protect oil fields from sabotage and political disturbances. "Using military forces to secure access to oil," he argued, "would involve the same gross under-estimate of the political-military challenge that we confronted in Vietnam." Some opponents assert that the very existence of a rapid-deployment force would create severe problems for Washington in the Gulf. In a letter to Carter in August 1979, Senator Mark O. Hatfield, Republican of Oregon, and twenty-six members of the House of Representatives argued that an interventionary force would "raise tensions in the area, jeopardize both the diplomacy of the region and the availability of its oil and,

perhaps most importantly, critically undermine the credibility of the United States as a peacemaker."

Following the Soviet intervention in Afghanistan, the
U.S. Administration accelerated plans to create the rapid-
development force. An important move in this direction was
Carter's request for a substantial increase in the Pentagon
budget, a good part of which was to be earmarked to the
proposed force.

Apart from creating a quick-reaction force for use in the
region, there was a compelling need to establish bases that
could be accessible to the United States in time of crisis.
Unlike the Soviet Union, which enjoyed the use of military
facilities in South Yemen and Ethiopia, the United States
disposed of no comparable installations. Dispatching units
from the Seventh Fleet in the Pacific from its base in Subic
Bay required over a week's time, much too long to allow
rapid intervention in the Gulf. As a result, the Administration assigned high priority to establishing a permanent naval
and air presence in the region. The United States kept a
small, three-ship force in the Persian Gulf at Bahrain, and
larger naval task forces periodically sail into the Indian
Ocean, using facilities at the British-owned island of Diego
Garcia, 2,500 miles southeast of the Persian Gulf. Given the
increasingly turbulent situation in the Persian Gulf that
could require American military action, the search for military bases or facilities had taken on great urgency. Actually,
there are North Atlantic Treaty Organization bases open to
the United States in Greece, Turkey and Italy. But not only
are these distant from the Gulf area, their employment by
forces destined for operations in the Gulf region could be
opposed by the nations involved on political, economic and
religious grounds.

A strong case for acquiring facilities had been building up
in the United States for some time. Military planners agreed
that it would be possible to land an adequate force in the
Gulf region in well under a week. But this force would come
from the United States, and all its follow-up equipment

would have to be flown in from the United States. In addition, base camps would have to be built and made secure and extra landing strips constructed. The establishment of a base or bases in the region would eliminate some of these difficulties. These bases would permit the storing of military equipment and other essentials. In times of comparative stability, they would serve as a home port for American ships and planes. Military planners have emphasized that such bases should not be considered as temporary expedients. As long as the United States remains dependent for a large share of its energy supplies on Gulf oil, it will have an interest in maintaining peace in the area. Whatever the base may cost, it has been argued, the long-term savings would be greater.

There have been, on the other hand, strong arguments against the acquisition of bases or facilities in the region. The governments of the Gulf region, although they desire an American presence to balance the potential Soviet threat to their security, do not want American forces on their soil. Arab rulers argue that any U.S. presence would inevitably lead to clashes between the Americans and the local populace that would be exploited by pro-Soviet agitators or nationalists. Some Americans sensitive to the delicate balance of Soviet-American relations have contended that the establishment of a base would upset that balance and provoke the Soviets to extend their influence, possibly by military means. Others have argued that the base would inevitably involve the United States in the tangled politics of the region and that the result would be American involvement in support of royal, right-wing governments with which the United States has little in common. A military argument is that there is no real need for the base and that frequent visits by powerful naval forces could prove sufficient to protect American interests. Politically, such a base, far from insuring stability in the long run, would have a destabilizing effect on the area. Any Arab suspicion of even convert Israeli assistance to the Americans would inflame the Arab world.

Notwithstanding criticism of the base program, there has been far more sentiment in favor of such a program. There has been a growing consensus in the United States that bases or facilities are necessary for the protection of American interests, which means the security of the oilfields and the oil shipping routes. From the outset of the base-acquisition program, five had been under active consideration. The first, the British-built complex at Mersa Metruh in Western Egypt, is considered too distant. Two possible sites are in Oman, one on Masira Island, off the coast. Until recently, the British Royal Air Force had maintained a base there, and it remains in good repair. The second site is in the port of Matrah, outside the Persian Gulf. In the early 1970s the Soviet Union established an important air and sea base at Berbera, in Somalia. Following the falling out between the two countries in 1978, the base has remained unused. Futher south, in Kenya is the strategic port of Mombasa.

In February 1980, the United States announced that it had concluded agreements with Oman, Kenya and Somalia giving American forces access to military facilities. In Oman, the chief American objective was to gain increased access to the airstrip on Marisa Island and to the port of Muscat. In Kenya, American ships had occasionally visited the port of Mombasa in the past and would now have access to the port and its facilities on an assured basis. Under the agreement with Somalia, the United States would enjoy access to Berbera. While the port itself was said to require repairs, a 15,000-foot runway nearby could be used by American planes. Not long after the announcement of the agreements, President Carter ordered an 1,800-man amphibious assault force into the Arabian Sea to demonstrate the ability of the United States to project ground forces into the Gulf region. Under terms of the agreements, each country is to receive a certain amount of arms and economic assistance in exchange for use of their facilities. Oman was promised about $100 million, Kenya $53 million and Somalia $45

million, not counting $111 million for refugee and develop-
ment aid in Somalia over the following two years.

For the United States, getting toeholds in East Africa had
been a sticky proposition from the start. Kenya would have
nothing to do with the idea until Washington promised that
it would not supply Somalia with offensive weapons. Moga-
dishu's idea of "Greater Somalia" includes a piece of north-
east Kenya, as well as the Ogaden region of Ethiopia. To
keep peace with most Africans, to avoid provoking Soviet-
backed Ethiopia, and to persuade Kenya to go along with
providing facilities in Mombassa, the State Department had
tried, in vain, to get Somalia to reverse its expansionist aims.
The Somali government did assert that no regular Somali
troops had been operating in the continuing conflict in
Ethiopia's Ogaden province. There were some misgivings in
Congress over the deal with Somalia because of reports that
units of its regular army were in action against Ethiopian
forces in the Ogaden. A Congressional subcommittee,
headed by Representative Stephen J. Solarz, Democrat of
New York, had expressed opposition to the agreement with
Somalia on the ground that the risk of being dragged into
conflict with the Soviet Union in the Horn of Africa out-
weighs Berbera's strategic attractions. Ethiopia's leader,
Lieutenant Colonel Mengistu Haile Mariam, had accused
the United States in September 1980 of colluding in Somali
aggression against his country.

After the overthrow of the shah, President Anwar al-
Sadat invited the United States to use bases and even to
station troops in Egypt. The motives behind this move were
not difficult to discern. Sadat was anxious to expand economic, political and military ties with Washington. Egypt
had already become a major recipient of economic and
military assistance from the United States following the
Camp David agreement. Egypt was also deeply concerned
over Soviet expansionism in the Red Sea area and its growing role in South Yemen and Ethiopia. Sadat, who had
expelled Soviet troops and advisers from his country in

1972, was said to be fearful that the Soviets, with their growing political and military strength in the Red Sea area, could undermine the moderate states. It was widely assumed that Southern Yemen's attack against Northern Yemen in early 1979, which posed a threat to Saudi Arabia, could not have occurred without the support of the Kremlin. Yet another purpose of Sadat's was to have Egypt replace Israel as America's most important ally in the Middle East. Because of Washington's differences with Prime Minister Menahem Begin's government over such issues as Jerusalem and the Palestinian talks, and, even more importantly, Egypt's strategic assets, there have been signs that Sadat's strategy of making his country into a preferred ally of the United States in the region, has had some success.

Under an agreement with the United States, Egypt has made available Ras Banas as a launching pad for American rapid-deployment forces. Ras Banas, a point of land extending into the Red Sea across from Saudia Arabia, would be improved to accommodate military planes and a division of troops. The planes and troops would not be stationed at Ras Banas permanently but instead would fly there during periods of tension in the Middle East. The Pentagon estimated that the cost of the construction work would range from $200 million to $400 million, with the higher figure likely to be nearer to the ultimate price tag. The airfield at Ras Banas is scheduled to be first class, with runways big enough to accommodate the largest transports and bombers. The investment in Ras Banas, coupled with joint exercises that have been held between units of the Egyptian and American air forces, point up the growing ties between the two countries and the growing Egyptian role in extending the U.S. reach in the Indian Ocean.

America's resolve to deploy military forces in the general Middle East area was strongly welcomed in Israel. For Israel, tiny and vulnerable and utterly dependent on the military resolve of the United States, the post-Vietnam aversion to projecting American power into distant crises has been particularly unsettling. Combined with the oil squeeze, and Washington's consequent sensitivity to Arab attitudes, it stirred up old fears of abandonment in a Jewish state founded after Western countries slammed their doors against so many Jews fleeing Hitler's Germany. Israelis have been fearful that Washington would force them to make too many concessions to the Palestinians and that such concessions might lead to the establishment of an independent Palestinian state beholden to the Soviet Union. On the world scene, the nightmare haunting many Israelis is the specter of an American military establishment unable or unwilling to stop Soviet expansionism.

Like a growing number of Americans, prominent Israelis have deplored the "emasculation" of American military intelligence services and Pentagon failure to keep pace with Soviet military growth. In the aftermath of the Iranian and Afghan crises, Israel has portrayed itself as strategically valuable to the United States. Experts say that an entire American division could land in an emergency and be fully outfitted immediately with American arms and equipment. Hugh depots with ammunition, spare parts, repair facilities and technicians could smooth American logistics. And the Russians know it, which may explain their spy ship stationed off the Israeli coast. Despite its small size, Israel sees itself as a spot of stability at the edge of a sea of Arab states with precarious leadership. The Saudi regime is seen as anachronistic, ultimately doomed to Islamic fundamentalism or, perhaps, leftist takeover. President Sadat of Egypt, it is argued by Israelis, is not immortal. His pro-American stance and commitment to peace with Israel may not survive him. King Hussein of Jordan is a minority figure ruling a population overwhelmingly Palestinian. Lebanon is occupied by Syrian troops and guerrillas of the Palestine Liberation Organization. And pro-Soviet Syria is torn by internal strife.

Against this background, Israel has argued that it is Washington's only dependable friend in the Middle East, proven by providing important intelligence, including computer analysis of Soviet weapons performance in combat and even captured Soviet weapons. On more than one occasion, Prime Minister Begin and former Defense Minister Ezer Weizman have made it clear that the United States was welcome to use Israeli ports and air bases.

Despite these generally acknowledged assets, the Carter Administration did not see fit to take up the Begin offer of bases. In good measure, this had been due to Egypt's superior geographic location, providing the precise constellation of factors needed for an American bridgehead in the Gulf region. Egyptian bases, and for that matter bases in Oman, Kenya and Somalia, would not have the embarrassing political repercussions for the United States that building a base in Haifa or Ashdod would have. A U.S. base in Israel would not only cause a further rift with Washington's Arab allies, such as Saudi Arabia and Jordan, but would virtually preclude any American overture to Iraq. The latter's importance has increased both because it has the second-largest reserves of oil in the Gulf area and because it lies at the heart of the region and has common borders with Iran, Syria, Jordan, Kuwait, Turkey and Saudi Arabia. The United States, moreover, has been pleased by Iraq's slow but definite movement away from the Soviet Union, with which it has a treaty of friendship.

In the light of these facts, Israel has met growing difficulties in arguing the thesis that it is of vital strategic importance to the United States. This has been evidenced by the virtual suspension of the joint consultations that had been held between American and Israeli military officials on strategic matters of common concern. It was further underscored in April 1980 when Israel was totally excluded from the unsuccessful effort to rescue American hostages in Iran. Despite the fact that Israel possessed perhaps the best intelligence on Iran, no request had been made for it. And its proven experience in missions of this kind was likewise ignored. Egypt, on the other hand, played a key role in the whole operation, both during its preparation and when it was put into action.

Outlook for U.S. Policy

With the enunciation of the so-called Carter Doctrine, the United States committed itself to a course of protecting the Persian Gulf through its own resources. It can no longer, as it did during the era of the shah's rule, depend on Iran to serve as its surrogate in the area. The shah's overthrow, along with subsequent developments in Iran and Afghanistan, signaled the demise of the Nixon Doctrine. The Carter Doctrine seeks to fill the military vacuum in the region with American power. Consistent with this new doctrine, the United States has been building up its own military forces for possible deployment in the region. At the same time, it has succeeded in securing access to military facilities in a number of strategically located, pro-Western countries within the region. These facilities are expected to enable the United States to establish a military presence in the region in time of crisis and, indirectly, strengthen these countries against possible external attack. And as part of the new Carter Doctrine, the United States has increased its naval presence in the Indian Ocean, ruling out, at least for the time being, any hope of demilitarizing this vast ocean.

While this new military posture is likely to secure Western access to Gulf oil from external attack, it is less certain that it can afford much protection against internal subversion or guerrilla threats which, many observers have argued, represent the most likely threats to stability within the region. There is also the possibility that the United States, as a consequence of the new political strategy, may become embroiled in local conflicts. And in the not unlikely event of Soviet intervention in Iran, the United States may become involved in a military confrontation with the Russians in an area where the terms of battle are likely to be dictated by the Kremlin. Such an intervention could come about in the event of Iran becoming fragmented. Such a scenario, along with possible others that could threaten American interests in the region, have obliged the United States to adopt a stronger policy for safeguarding the Persian Gulf with all that may imply for direct military intervention.

War in the Gulf: The Iran-Iraq Conflict

Iraq: Attack on Iran

On September 9, 1980, the uneasy peace between Iran and Iraq was shattered when Iraqi President Saddam Hussein sent his troops marching across the Iranian border. One army invaded Iran along the central border area closest to Baghdad, and another across the Shatt al Arab waterway into Khuzistan, Iran's oil-rich province. The Iraqi advance had been less than spectacular at first but was in accordance with an elementary and coherent strategy: clear the Shatt al Arab waterway, capture the oil port of Khurramshahr and Abadan and engage the remaining Iranian forces as far east of the frontier as possible. Six weeks after the attack, the slow but methodic plan of battle of the invaders had resulted in the taking of Khurramshahr and the virtual encirclement of Abadan, site of a huge Iranian oil refinery. Hussein's strategy of laying seige to the oilfields, which would cut off the Iranian economy from its lifeblood and Teheran from its fuel and cooking oil, appeared to be working.

The weakened Iranian forces, which had put up a far stiffer fight than the Iraqi generals had anticipated, were no match for the better disciplined and led Iraqis. Reports from Western intelligence sources showed that the Iranian defense was being conducted in the early crucial days of battle without any strategic or tactical control. Isolated battalions and companies were launching attacks or withdrawing from action without reference to a coherent operational plan. Iran's military establishment, confronted by its first serious challenge since the overthrow of the shah, was not up to the task of taking on the superior Iraqi army. In this first but crucial phase of the fighting, the country was paying the price for the government's purge of the military, which had been left demoralized and cut off from its American source of arms and spare parts.

Causes of the War

Although the war had been largely unexpected, it did not come as a complete surprise. Tension between Baghdad and Teheran had been building since the Ayatollah Khomeini came to power in Iran. Just prior to the Iraqi invasion, there were numerous border incidents involving troops and planes of both countries. The Iraqi leadership, headed by the tough President Hussein, had viewed Khomeini's achievement of power as both a threat and an opportunity. The threat was that it could encourage Iraq's millions of Shi'ites, who comprise a majority of Iraq's population, to turn against Hussein. The latter headed a socialist and secular government, which had felt increasingly vulnerable as the revolutionary forces of Islam spread through the Middle East. Iraq's leaders, drawn mostly from the Sunnite branch of Islam, had become deeply suspicious of the intentions of the revolutionary government in Teheran. Baghdad feared that Khomeini, who had mobilized millions of Iranian Shi'ites against the shah, would stir up Iraq's Shi'ite masses, many of whom felt excluded from political power. As tension between Iraq and Iran mounted, the Iranian revolutionary authorities stridently called for the overthrow of Hussein.

Compounding the fears of Baghdad was internal opposition from an assortment of groups, including intellectuals and communists, who resented the Ba'ath's dictatorial rule. In 1978, the government had executed a score of communists for allegedly promoting political activity in the army. There was also the problem of the Kurds, who had long sought greater autonomy. In 1975, Baghdad had succeeded in crushing the long Kurdish revolt with the cooperation of Iran under the shah. With Khomeini in power, there were reports of Iranian arms reaching the Kurds. The growing Kurdish opposition to Khomeini had also served to inspire Iraq's increasingly restive Kurdish population. As if to underscore the government's uncertain position, Hussein announced in July 1979 that he had foiled an attempted coup and that twenty-one officials, including prominent political and trade union leaders, at least four of whom were Shi'ites, had been executed by firing squad.

While the Iraqi leadership viewed, uneasily, the developments in neighboring Iran, it indicated that it felt threatened by the Egyptian-Israeli peace agreement. With Cairo opting out of the war with Israel, Syria stood alone against the Jewish state. The agreement also presented Baghdad with the prospect of the Israeli army streaming eastward across the desert to Iraq. As a result of these developments, Saddam Hussein gradually moved his country away from its long hard-line isolation within the region. The Egyptian-Israeli agreement, which led to Sadat's isolation within the Arab world, prompted Hussein to try to fill this political vacuum. Iraq, which, after Saudi Arabia, had become the second largest exporter of oil, and whose reserves of this resource were thought to be greater those of the Saudis, moved on a number of diplomatic fronts to assert its leadership in both the Arab world and in the Persian Gulf. President Hussein's initiatives in these two arenas were inextricably linked to one another.

Iraq's first move was to replace Egypt as leader of the anti-Israel coalition by serving as host for an anti-Sadat summit conference in October 1978. At this meeting it scored a diplomatic coup by reconciling hardliners, such as Libya, with moderates, notably Saudi Arabia, to agree to joint action against the Egyptian leader for his withdrawal from the war against Israel. The Iraqis moved to bury the decade-old hatchet cleaving the rival Ba'ath parties of Iraq and Syria that rule in Baghdad and Damascus (where the Ba'ath party is known as the Arab Socialist Resurrectionist Party). This process started in October 1978 with a surprise visit to Baghdad by Syrian President Hafiz al-Assad. The two countries announced the formation of a "Joint Political Command" that would work toward the unification of Ba'ath party affairs, constitutions and the military establishments. Although prospects for unification were not considered bright, the rapprochement between these two bitterly opposed countries was by itself considered a significant developments. It reduced Syria's political isolation and strengthened Saddam Hussein's claim for leadership in the Arab world. The Iraqi president also succeeded in making up with Jordan's King Hussein—only a year previously branded as an imperialist tool but now greeted as a "distinguished guest."

Along another, and more important, political front, the Iraqis moved to patch up relations with Saudi Arabia. For years, the latter had feared the radical, Soviet-aligned government in Baghdad. The Iraqis, in turn, scorned the Saudi princes as lackeys of the United States. This animosity between the two countries showed signs of changing after the overthrow of the shah. Both Baghdad and Riyadh, for reasons of their own, were unhappy with Islamic government in Teheran. Both felt threatened by it, and both feared that the revolutionary chaos inside Iran could promote instability in the Persian Gulf and, eventually, Soviet intervention. One of the first tangible signs of the improved relations between radical Iraq and conservative Saudi Ara-

bia was the little-publicized security coordination accord
that was intended to promote stability in the Gulf. As relations between the two countries have warmed up, the Saudis
have cautiously looked to Iraq as a partner in promoting
stability in the region and keeping radical forces at bay.
Significantly, Iraq refused to take part in the Confrontation
Front, formed by Libya's mercurial President Qadaffi, and
which included Algeria, Syria, South Yemen and the Palestine Liberation Organization. Coincidental with this, President Hussein moved closer to the mainstream elements in
the PLO by ending his dispute with the main guerrilla group
Al Fatah which had erupted in a worldwide series of assassi-
nations in 1978.

Iraq's Emergence as a Regional Power

With relations greatly improved with its once hostile Arab
neighbors, and with opposition elements inside the government purged, the Iraqi regime of President Saddam Hussein
took a number of measures to establish Iraq as the foremost
power in the Persian Gulf. A secret circular to Ba'ath party
members dated February 19, 1979, outlined some of the
hopes and fears that have fueled Iraq's new regional policy.
Dealing with the situation created by the fall of the shah, it
said: "The lake of oil seems now to be on the brink of a
volcano, and everybody is looking around, fearful for their
positions and future—except for Iraq, which is strong and
confident in itself and in its future. And this enables Iraq to
play the main role in stabilizing the region. . . . " Part of this
new role as a stabilizing force had developed even before the
dramatic developments had unfolded in Iran. This had to do
with Baghdad's decision to alter its relationship with the
superpowers. Under this policy of realignment, Baghdad
sharply downgraded its relations with Moscow and cautiously improved ties with the United States, with which it
had had no diplomatic ties since 1967.

In 1972, Iraq had signed a fifteen-year Treaty of Friendship & Cooperation with the Soviet Union. The Baghdad

government viewed the Soviets as natural allies in view of their own socialist proclivities and of Moscow's support of the Palestine cause and its opposition to U.S. policies in the Middle East. Washington had long been condemned by Iraq for its support of Israel; Iraq was the most implacable enemy of Jerusalem and had vowed never to make peace with it. In line with its close relations with Moscow, Iraq purchased virtually all of its weapons from the Soviet Union and was tied to it by close trade relations as well. After signing the treaty, Iraqi communists were allowed to function openly, even joining a national front.

This pro-Moscow orientation began to change within a few years. By the mid-1970s, Iraq had begun opening up to the West and curtailing its cooperation with the communist bloc. In June 1978, a member of the Iraqi cabinet declared that his country had decided to diverisfy its arms sources to ensure "freedom of action and decision." That month Defense Minister Yvon Bourges of France visited Iraq and reported that Baghdad had expressed interest in buying a ground defense system and "Crotale" surface-to-air missiles. Iraq's purchase diversification program had begun earlier in the economic sphere. Since 1975, important contracts for Iraqi development projects, which in the past had gone almost exclusively to Soviet-bloc organizations, were now going to American or West European companies. Soviet investment in Iraq had dropped to one-quarter of what it had been in 1972. Rubbing salt into Soviet wounds, Iraqi officials declared repeatedly that they want the best technology that money can buy. And with its huge oil revenues Iraq can afford to acquire precisely that.

Baghdad's action of veering away from its erstwhile ally, although not breaking with it, was motivated by a number of factors. The country's leaders were worried by the installation of a communist regime in Afghanistan in April 1978 soon after the rise of a Marxist government in Ethiopia. The discovery of communist cells inside the Iraqi army intensified these worries. Responding harshly to this development, the government ordered the execution of twenty-one members of the Soviet-supported Iraqi Communist Party. The Baghdad government roundly condemned the Soviet invasion of Afghanistan. Shortly after the Soviet intervention, *Al Thawra*, the newspaper of the ruling Ba'ath party, denounced Moscow's "flagrant intervention" in Afghanistan's internal affairs and urged the Kremlin to revise its Middle East policy, which, the paper said, was "based on converting the region into believing in Marxist ideology." The Baghdad daily also criticized Soviet influence in South Yemen and Ethiopia. It charged that the Soviet refusal to supply Arabs with advanced weapons had led to defeat by Israel in 1967 and 1973, and it criticized what it described as Soviet inability to respond to the Arabs' development needs, even when they paid immediately and in hard currency. Ba'athist and communist ideologies, moreover, were seen in Baghdad as incompatible. The Ba'athists advocate pan-Arab nationalism, a union of Arab states and a home-grown socialism opposed to Marxism in its international and proletarian aspects.

As relations with the Soviet Union declined, ties to the West improved. Trade with the United States has grown considerably, and the familiar shrill tone of Iraq's anti-American rhetoric has moderated. Nevertheless, Baghdad has refused to renew diplomatic ties with Washington, broken since the 1967 Arab-Israeli war, because of continued U.S. support of Israel. (Iraq was reportedly preparing to resume relations in 1977 after a high-ranking State Department official visited the country. The discussions fell through when the Iraqis were angered by a remark of President Carter referring to their country as a Soviet sphere of influence). Iraq has remained fearful of American intentions in the Persian Gulf region and has expressed strong opposition to big-power interference in the region. The Iraqi authorities have expressed strong oppostion to Soviet actions in Afghanistan, Southern Yemen and Ethiopia and have shown unhappiness over the growing U.S. naval presence in the Persian Gulf. Concern over "imperialist designs" in this oil-producing region has been directed equally at Moscow and Washington. Such an approach is understandable in the light of Iraq's own intentions of becoming a foremost regional power. A strong role by one or both superpowers could jeopardize Iraq's own aspirations and threaten its interests.

Iraq Goes to War

It is against these diplomatic developments that one must consider Baghdad's decision to go to war against Iran. The ruler of Iraq, President Saddam Hussein, had ambitions to make his country the acknowledged regional power, assuming, in effect, the role that the shah had successfully played for a number of years. As an Arab country championing Arab unity and the cause of the Palestinians, Hussein was no less anxious to establish himself as the ideological successor of the late Egyptian President Gamal Abdel Nasser by rallying the Arab world around the flag of pan-Arabism.

After it launched its invasion of Iran, Iraq denounced the border agreement that it had signed with the shah in 1975. Speaking in an interview with the French newspaper *Le Monde* as Iraqi forces kept up their pressure on the beseiged Iranian oil cities, First Deputy Prime Minister Taha Yasin Ramadan stressed that Iraq's ultimate aim was "to force Iran to recognize our rights and respect them." These he defined as full sovereignty over the Shatt al Arab waterway, which separates the two countries at the head of the Persian Gulf, and a redefinition of the border in the Musian area two hundred miles to the north. He also reiterated an Iraqi demand that three islands at the mouth of the Persian Gulf seized by the shah in 1971 be returned to "Arab sovereignty." Asked what would happen to Iran's oil if Iraqi forces succeeded in capturing Abadan, Khurramshahr and other cities in Khuzistan, Ramadan replied: "It will become Iraqi until a solution arises." At another point, he said: The Ayatollah Khomeini had previously declared that Iran

would not negotiate to end the fighting until the last Iraqi soldier left the country—a condition that President Hussein firmly rejected.

Deputy Prime Minister Ramadan's remark about "Arabistan," the name frequently used by Arabs in referring to the Iranian province of Khuzistan, provoked specluation in Washington that seizure of this oil-rich province was one of Iraq's ultimate aims. The status of Khuzistan has long been a sore point between Iran and Iraq. Under the Ottoman Empire, parts of the region as it then existed were held by what are now known as Iran, Iraq and Kuwait; after World War I, Britain attached it all to Iran. In 1960, Iraq began a campaign to break off the province and formed an "Al Ahwaz National Popular Front." In 1969 Saddam Hussein, then a young nationalist leader in the Ba'ath party, made Khuzistan a major target of his anti-Iranian campaign, and nearly 6,000 Arabs from there were recruited and trained in Iraq. But as part of the 1975 agreement between Iran and Iraq, the latter dropped its claims to the region. Ramadan's remarks about holding on to the region's oil could be interpreted as an attempt by President Hussein to revive Iraq's claim to the entire province, a majority of whose population is Arab. This raised the specter of a partial dismemberment of Iran, which could set in motion centrifugal forces in the country. The implications of this in terms of the regional balance of power and U.S.-Soviet interests were not lost on the United States.

The U.S. & the War

When the Iraqi-Iranian conflict broke out, American policy was one of neutrality. Lacking any leverage on either side, the Carter Administration expressed hope for a quick end to the fighting and to limiting its possible spread. High priority was given to preventing the Soviet Union from spreading its influence in the area. There was, moreover, no immediate concern about the impact of the war on the oil situation; at the time, the Western industrial countries had more than a 100-day supply on hand, and the Saudis had promised that they would increase production by a million barrels a day as a partial offset to the loss of the combined Iranian-Iraqi production, which had been in excess of three million barrels.

As a result, the Carter Administration decided to avoid any show of force. An American naval fleet, consisting of two carrier battle groups, stayed in the Arabian Sea, while diplomats urged Arab and other nations, including the Soviet Union, to exercise restraint and to press the belligerents to accept a cease-fire. American officials were particularly concerned that Moscow might exploit the situation by either moving closer to Iraq or by gaining a foothold in Iran if it were defeated. By coincidence, American Secretary of State Edmund Muskie had a long-scheduled meeting with Foreign Minister Andrei A. Gromyko of the Soviet Union in New York September 25, 1980. The occasion was used to gain a pledge by the superpowers of nonintervention in the conflict. Muskie was said to have told his Soviet counterpart that it was in the interests of both countries to adopt a hand-off policy. Gromyko reportedly gave Muskie a pledge from Soviet President Brezhnev affirming a policy of nonintervention.

Events soon overtook these developments. Late in the evening of September 26, the U.S. Central Intelligence Agency received an urgent message from its station chief in Saudi Arabia saying that Saudi leaders, anxious about a possible attack from Iran, wanted prompt American military help, although they did not specify the nature of the help sought. The Saudis were alarmed becuase they had allowed some Iraqi planes to land on their airfields and had permitted other Iraqi planes to fly through their airspace to Oman. The Iranians had warned publicly that they might retaliate against any country aiding Iraq. While the kind of assistance to be sent was being discussed, senior Carter Administration officials had to confront another serious problem. American and British intelligence reported that Iraqi helicopters and planes were preparing to use facilities in Oman and Saudi Arabia to attack bases in Iran across the Persian Gulf and on three Iranian-held islands.

The Saudi message precipitated a sharp division of opinion between national security adviser Brzezinski and Secretary of State Muskie.

Some national security staff members had favored adopting a strong response. The suggested strong response included proposals for the dispatch to Saudi Arabia of two F-14 squadrons, about forty planes, from the carrier *Eisenhower* in the Arabian Sea and, from the United States, a similar number of F-15s as well as advanced Hawk air defense missile batteries with American crews. Some military officers saw in the situation an opportunity to gain Saudi assent to earlier American proposals for closer military cooperation. The Pentagon had been pressing the Saudis to allow the stockpiling of equipment at air bases that could be used by American forces in the event of a major war in the region. The Saudis, while supporting the U.S. efforts to strengthen the American military presence elsewhere in the area, had been wary of such direct collaboration.

In contrast, Secretary Muskie and his aides, concerned about Arab sensitivities and about maintaining the neutrality of both Moscow and Washington in the Persian Gulf war, were said to be wary of the United States' becoming too deeply involved. Muskie reportedly took this tack because he was concerned about the impact that a major American military move might have on professed American neutrality in the conflict and about how the Soviet Union might perceive the situation. He said at the meeting that he did not want to do anything that might be inconsistent with what he had told Gromyko just a few days earlier. It was tentatively agreed that, while the United States needed to demonstrate its concern for Saudi security, it would be a mistake to introduce any offensive military systems into the conflict. In consequence of that decision, the Administration announced

September 29 that it had decided to send four radar warning planes to Saudi Arabia.

The dispatch of these defensive planes, in the view of some experts, has brought the United States even closer to supporting Saudi Arabia in a way not anticipated by the Carter Doctrine. Under that doctrine, President Carter declared that the United States was prepared to use military force to protect oil supplies in the Persian Gulf from external threats. But the United States, in responding to Saudi Arabia's concern over becoming embroiled in the Iranian-Iraqi war, may have gone a step further in raising the possibility of injecting American military power in internal regional conflicts to assure a continued flow of oil.

As the fighting dragged on, the Carter Administration became increasingly concerned over Iraq's ultimate war aims. Although deeply preoccupied by the situation of the American hostages held by Iran, the Administration feared that an Iraqi victory could lead to the dismemberment of Iran. There were signs of a subtle tilt by Washington toward the Iranians. Following Iraqi Deputy Prime Minister Ramadan's remark about Arabistan (Khuzistan) and its oil, the State Department cautioned Iraq that "it could not condone" the seizure of Iran's oil-producing province. Barely a fortnight after the outbreak of the war, Warren M. Christopher, the Deputy Secretary of State, expressing concern that the Iranian-Iraqi conflict was spreading beyond original estimates, disclosed in a television interview that although the United States remained neutral in the Persian Gulf conflict, this did not mean that Washington would countenance any drastic changes in the situation brought about by Iraqi moves into Iran. "We certainly would be strongly opposed to any dismemberment of Iran," he said. Although the United States had severe problems with Iran over the American hostages, Christopher seemed to suggest that at the moment Washington was more concerned about an overwhelming Iraqi victory than about anything else in the conflict.

Several weeks later, Secretary of State Muskie, in offering a two-point proposal to bring an end to the war, stated that "we are opposed to the dismemberment of Iran." In the same speech, he referred to Iraq's action in Iran as an "invasion" and warned that it threatened the stability of the whole Persian Gulf region. Muskie affirmed the official American position of impartiality in the struggle. But he said that "to be impartial is not to be inactive; to declare that we will not take sides is not to declare that we have no interest at stake." He then went on to state that "the integrity of Iran is today threatened by the Iraqi invasion." The Secretary of State and other senior American officials repeated assurances that when Iran released the hostages, the United States would act quickly to dismantle the system of international economic and political sanctions erected against Iran. The end of the American effort to isolate Iran would enable Teheran to resume large-scale trade with Western Europe and Japan. It might also allow Iran to begin receiving four hundred million dollars worth of military spare parts that had been bought from the United States.

Statements by Carter Administration officials indicating that spare parts could be sold to Iran if the hostages were released drew critical comments in Republican quarters. Some Republicans argued that the President might be pursuing a conciliatory line toward Teheran in the hope of gaining quick release of the hostages, a development that could strengthen his bid for reelection. Former Secretary of State Henry A. Kissinger complained that the Administration was in danger of taking an overly conciliatory line toward Teheran. He expressed concern that Washington, by appearing too eager to meet any conditions laid down by Khomeini, could lose respect in foreign capitals. Rebutting this point of view, a White House national security specialist contended that an end to the hostage crisis could enhance Washington's "freedom of action" in the Persian Gulf by permitting planners to focus on the long-range goal of strengthening the American military presence in the area.

As the war continued, U.S. national security adviser Brezezinski and other officials had become increasingly concerned about Iran's fate and the war's implications for regional stability. One concern has been that Iraq's military foothold in Khuzistan could foster political turbulence in other parts of the country that could be exploited by the Soviet Union. There had also been concern that Iraq could try to absorb Khuzistan. Discussing this possibility, some experts asserted that the province could become a permanent point of tension and fighting, like the dispute between Israel and Jordan over the West Bank. Some officials held that if Washington could normalize ties with Teheran, Iraq would become more amenable to seeking a negotiated settlement to the conflict. This was based on the view that an important factor in Iraq's orginial decision to go to war was Iran's political isolation and its inabiity to obtain spare parts for its largely U.S.-equipped military machine. Another point of view was that a resolution of the hostage crisis might work to prolong the fighting if the Iranians believed that an end to Western sanctions would give their armed forces a new lease on life.

The War's Impact on the Stability of the Region

As long as the war continued, there remained the strong possibility of its spreading to other parts of the Gulf area. The United States and other Western powers, notably Britain and France, had assembled an armada of ships near the Gulf to ensure that the Straits of Hormuz remained open to international shipping. Should American ships intervene against either side, this could invite a Soviet response. The possibility of superpower confrontation, although seriously reduced as a result of the Soviet and American pledges of nonintervention, could arise in the not-to-distant future in the event the war dragged on. The United States might feel compelled to expand its military role in protecting Saudi Arabia. As the United States increased its capacity to project military power in the region, the possibility of such intervention would grow. For its part, the Soviet Union, concerned about the growing disarray along its southern borders, might be tempted to send in troops under the pretext of restoring order in Iran.

The war had already posed a serious challenge to American diplomacy in the region. Although there was little love lost between Washington and Teheran, the United States remained opposed to any Iraqi actions that would result in the dismemberment of Iran. There were signs that the Carter Administaration wanted to restore normal ties with Iran, and the Carter Administration hinted that it would be willing to ship spare parts for the badly battered Iranian military forces. However, as long as the politically divided government in Teheran failed to release the American hostages, no improvement in relations was possible. Should the United States send spare parts to Iran once the hostage issue was resolved, this would seriously strain relations between the Americans and the Iraqis, and with the Saudis as well. Riyadh, along with a number of other Arab regimes, tacitly backed Iraq and would be expected to oppose anything that smacked of U.S.-Iranian cooperation. The United States, as a result, was impaled on the horns of a diplomatic dilemma. To provide aid to Iran would incur the wrath of Iraq and its Arab allies; not to do so, could lead to a decisive Iraqi victory that could well result in Baghdad becoming the foremost regional power in the Gulf. An Iranian defeat could then set the stage for Soviet intervention in this country, and this could lead to a U.S.-Soviet confrontation.

(Since Iran did not free the hostages until the very day Carter's successor was inaugurated as U.S. President, the Carter Administration never had to reach the decision about the military shipments.)

In regional terms, the war could be expected to have a destabilizing effect on the entire Persian Gulf area for a considerable time to come. The oil-producing capacity of both countries, particularly Iran, was hard hit by the fighting. It would take vast sums of money and considerable time to repair this damage. Politically, relations between the countries were certain to remain strained even after peace

was restored. Iran was not likely to forget or forgive its
neighbor for its aggressive behavior, particularly if Baghdad
held on to any territory. There was mounting concern in the
United States that the Iraqis harbored designs on the oil-
producing Khuzistan province.

The war served to deepen the divisions in the Arab world,
with the more radical states, notably Syria, Libya and Algeria, backing the Iranians, and the conservative ones supporting Iraq. It was assumed that the latter group of countries,
led by Saudi Arabia, would probably be less than happy if
Iraq were to achieve a decisive military victory. Such an
outcome would make them vulnerable to increased pressures from Baghdad, whose ultimate aims in the Persian
Gulf had remained suspect in the Arab monarchies in the
region. Arab states supporting Iran had also shown a certain
wariness toward the conflict. Syria, despite the break in
relations with Iraq, kept open a pipeline carrying Iraqi oil to
the Mediterranean. In contrast to this cautious behavior,
Libya denounced Saudi Arabia for allowing American
planes to be stationed there, stating that by this decision the
Saudis had forfeited their rights as custodians of the holy
Arab shrines. Outraged by this attack, Riyadh severed ties
with Libya. The war has also had an adverse effect on the
standing of the Palestine Liberation Organization. Ideologically, there was strong support within the PLO, particularly
among its more leftist groups, for the Ayatollah Khomeini,
who, on coming to power, proclaimed unreserved backing
of the Palestinian cause. To give expression to these senti-
ments, however, would have caused the PLO to forfeit much
support in the Arab world which was antagonistic to the
Khomeini revolution. Should the PLO have continued to
remain neutral, it risked losing the considerable goodwill it
had within the Iranian ruling establishment. The PLO's role
in the conflict did not endear it to Iraq, which could argue
that the Palestinians had a moral obligation to support
fellow Arabs. Apart from these considerations, the Persian
Gulf war distracted world attention from the Palestine ques-

tion, which, until then, had enjoyed a high priority on the United Nations agenda.

These divisions played into the hands of Israel. A divided Arab world reduced the possibilities of an Arab attack against Israel and blocked unity in Arab pressure for the creation of a Palestinian state. The short-term benefits of the war were obvious. Neither Iraq nor Iran, weakened by the conflict, would be able to commit their military and economic resources in a war against the Jewish state for the foreseeable future. Politically, the Israelis could argue that the threat to Persian Gulf and Middle East oil emanated not from their position on the Palestine issue or on Jerusalem but from the Arab states themselves. This argument could carry weight in American political circles and reduce pressure on any Israeli government to make concessions to the Palestinians. Endemic rivalries within the Arab world and the opportunities that these rivalries present to the Soviet Union to make political gains might well absorb the attention of the Administration of the newly elected President Ronald Reagan.

Whatever else the Iran-Iraq war demonstrated, it clearly revealed American weakness in the region. Lacking leverage with either belligerent, the United States was helpless to stop the war and the great damage it caused to oil fields and refining installations. Nor was it certain that the military measures the United States adopted could prevent the conflict from spreading. Much the same can be said for the Soviet Union. It had no reason to see the war continue, and yet it lacked the power to bring it to an end. Moscow, undecided as to which side to back, decided to steer clear of the conflict, probably hoping that it would wind down in a manner that would result in disadvantage to both sides. No matter how the conflict ended, the superpowers would have to reassess their past policies and future prospects in this strategic and highly unstable part of the world.

Index

DATE DUE

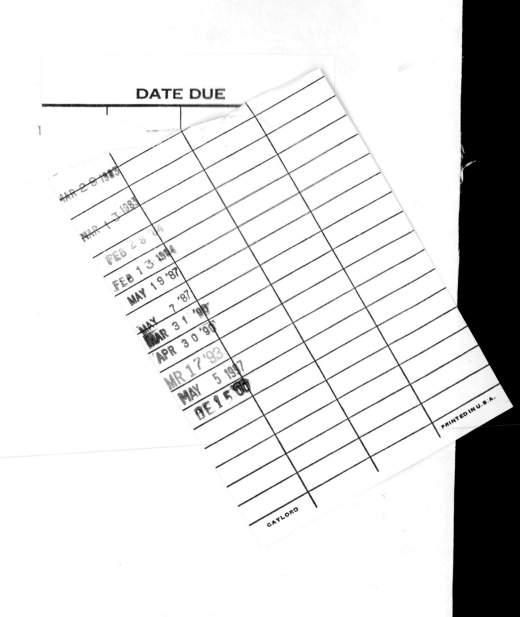

MAR 29 1983

MAR 1 3 1983

FEB 2 8 '84

FEB 1 3 1984

MAY 19 '87

MAY 7 '87

MAY 31 '90

MAR 30 '90

APR 30 '90

MR 17 '93

MAY 5 1997

DE 15 00

GAYLORD

PRINTED IN U.S.A.